Children working as station porters in Lwow, Poland 1936.

First published in 2000 by
Bradford Heritage Recording Unit
in association with the
Migration & Ethnicity Research Centre at the University of Sheffield.

All rights reserved.
ISBN: 0-907734-57-X

Copyright © 2000

For the photographs: BHRU, Sikorski Museum, Imperial War Museum, the Integrated and Applied Crop Research Centre at Rothemstead, Weiner Library, West Yorkshire Archive Service, National Museums of Scotland, David King Collection, Walter Scotts, Tim Smith, Janina Struk.

For the texts: Michelle Winslow, BHRU, British Library National Sound Archive, University of Sheffield.

Extracts from interviews were not necessarily said by people who appear in the photographs that accompany them.

Acknowledgements.

It would be impossible to name all those who have helped us with this book. Our interviews are conducted on the basis of maintaining confidentiality, and we would like to thank all those who have shared their memories with us.

Some individuals and organisations do merit special thanks.

For their help, advice and loan of material: Witold Szablewski, Barbara Szablewska, Thomas Wachowiak, Leon Rodowicz-Rutowicz, Zygmunt Zaleski, Krzysztof Barbarski, Czeslaw Zychowicz, Graham Smith, Barbara Stepien-Foad, Barbara Woroncow, Janina Struk, Wolodymyr Demtschuk, Rob Perks, Olive Howarth, Lubomir Jovanovich, Jan Godbold, Carol Greenwood, Anthea Stephenson, Peter Jackson, Colin Holmes, Richard Jenkins, and staff at the Sikorski Museum and the Imperial War Museum photographic library.

For the use of interview material: The British Library National Sound Archive.

For funding: Marks and Spencer and the Polonia Aid Foundation Trust.

Editorial Assistant: Janet Collopy.

Photographic prints: Katrina Bajic.

Design: S2 01977 712362

Printing: Thornton & Pearson 01484 727135

A police officer, and his son now living in Sheffield, have their portrait taken in a studio in Warsaw in the 1930s.

BHRU.

Keeping The Faith

The Polish Community In Britain

Tim Smith
Michelle Winslow

Bradford Heritage Recording Unit
in association with the University of Sheffield

View of Krakow in the late 1930s. Once Poland's ancient royal capital, it is one of the architectural gems of Central Europe.

INTRODUCTION

The Polish community in Britain is one of the biggest minority communities in the country. Little is known outside the Polish community about how and why they came to Britain, and how their community-in-exile has developed over the past sixty years. This book documents the history of the Polish people who have made Britain their home.

A small number of Polish-born people lived in Britain before 1939. However it was the traumatic events of the Second World War, and the political settlements with which it ended, that brought 160,000 Christian - overwhelmingly Roman Catholic - Poles to Britain. *Keeping the Faith* focuses on these people and their descendants. Although some Ukrainians and Jews who came to Britain after the War were actually born in Poland, they tended to identify with their own community organisations, and their story is a different one.

Beginning with the Nazi invasion of Poland in 1939, the web of stories woven by the lives of hundreds of thousands of people is a complex one. This book gives voice to some of them, using extracts from interviews with Poles who settled in this country, and their children and grandchildren. The roots of this project go back to 1984, when the Bradford Heritage Recording Unit (BHRU) began an oral history programme tape-recording the life stories, memories and reflections of three generations of local Poles. Their photographs and documents were archived, and new photographs taken recording their contemporary lives.

Many of the older generation spoke at length of the events of the War years and their aftermath. That period occupies a large proportion of this book because it was a pivotal time for Poles, one which was to change their lives absolutely. The interviewees also spoke of their uncompromising stand since the War, refusing to travel to Poland or to have any contact with the Warsaw regime. Although the collapse of Communism in Europe then seemed an unrealistic dream, they expressed their hopes for a free and independent Poland to which they might one day return.

This dream became reality when in August 1989, after nearly a decade of extraordinary changes, Poland appointed its first non-Communist leader since the War. Since Poland's independence, research work with the Polish community in Britain has expanded. Michelle Winslow of the Migration and Ethnicity Research Centre at the University of Sheffield, and Tim Smith of BHRU, went on to interview and photograph Polish people throughout the country. The book combines new and archive material with images from photographic collections, notably those of the Imperial War Museum and the Sikorski Museum in London, which houses the military and political records of the Polish government-in-exile.

The journeys which people made from Poland to this country are many and varied. A great number survived truly horrific events, and much of what they experienced defies description. When journalist Ed Murrow witnessed the liberation of Buchenwald concentration camp - which held many Poles - in 1945, he stated: 'I pray you to believe what I have said. I reported what I saw and heard, but only part of it. For most of it I have no words'.

Many of our interviewees also struggled to find the words to describe their experiences during the War. Often they would resort to asking 'Can you imagine?'. Although it is almost impossible for outsiders to imagine what life was like during these times, we hope that this book provides a small but fitting testament to people's experiences and to the community they went on to build in Britain.

Map of Poland showing borders before and after the Second World War.

BACKGROUND

Where does Poland begin and end? This is a question which has occupied both Poles and their neighbours throughout the turbulent history of central Europe. A hundred years ago Poland had disappeared from the map, yet today it lies at the political and military heart of Europe. A lack of natural boundaries, with only the Baltic Sea to the north and the Carpathian mountains to the south, has given the area a complex history.

Historians put the founding of the original Polish state as 966. At this time tribal groups in the region were settling down to form relatively stable kingdoms. One of these tribes, the Polane, had established themselves in the lands around Poznan and northwards along the River Vistula up to the Baltic Sea. In 966 their leader, King Miesko I, adopted the western form of Christianity. Over the centuries that followed Poland grew into a large and powerful multi-ethnic state cemented by marriages between its royal family and that of Lithuania. In 1569, Poland and its northern ally Lithuania formed a single 'Commonwealth' with a united parliament, ruling lands from the Baltic to the Black Sea, and binding together races with many different origins, languages and cultures. Although the ruling classes throughout this Polish-Lithuanian Commonwealth became 'polonised' (and the Poles still regard present day Vilnius, the capital of Lithuania, as an ancient Polish city), it was the state's diversity and size that brought about its downfall. The government used a system of 'Liberum Veto', where a single vote in its Parliament of Nobles could act as a veto. With so many disparate groups represented in Parliament, it was difficult to pass legislation or to raise taxes, particularly to payroll an army capable of fending off the territorial ambitions of its neighbours.

By the end of the eighteenth century Poland had completely disappeared, dismantled in stages by its powerful and traditional enemies. The Russians ruled over Russian Poland in the east, the Germans incorporated the central area into Prussia, and the Austrians made Krakow, Lwow and the surrounding regions part of their Austro-Hungarian Empire. People living in each of these occupied areas were caught in a complicated web of loyalties. But for many the idea of Poland as a nation - a community of people sharing common ideas of their culture and origins - continued to thrive.

This belief in Poland was expressed through opposition to the ruling states, particularly in areas ruled by the Germans and the Russians where Polish language and culture were suppressed, and uprisings brutally put down. The idea of Poland became closely identified with the Roman Catholic Church (as against the German Protestantism or Russian Orthodoxy of the rulers). Against this background of intense faith the idea of Poland as a collective Christ arose, crucified by its oppressors, but which would one day be resurrected. While the masses knelt before the Virgin Mary, Queen of Poland, stories of a glorious Polish past were kept alive by the intelligentsia. These old ideas still contribute greatly to the sense of drama and tragedy in Poland's history and politics, and even influenced the development of the Polish community in Britain.

Poland appeared on the map again in 1918, its rulers having collapsed in revolution or defeat at the end of the First World War. However after generations of living under separate rulers, the idea of Poland did not match the reality. Its people were culturally diverse and ethnic groups were intermingled. In some places Poles were in the majority, in others a minority. As well as 22 million Poles, in the eastern provinces there were five million Ukrainians, 1.5 million Byelorussians, and large numbers of Lithuanians and Russians. In the west lived 700,000 Germans. Nearly a third of the population in towns and cities were Jewish, who spoke Yiddish as their first language.

A senior engineer involved with the railways is photographed with his family in their garden in Czernowitz, July 1912. *West Yorkshire Archive Service*.

Family standing next to the village well in Chrostowy, near Krakow, 1936. *IACRC*.

Woman on the steps of her farmhouse in Berezie, a village in eastern Poland, 1936. *IACRC*.

King Sigismund's square in Warsaw, the capital of Poland, in the 1930s. *IACRC*.

Pre-war view of Warsaw, capital city of Poland.

Sikorski Museum.

The nation needed rebuilding and the challenge was taken up by Josef Pilsudski, the authoritarian Commander-in-Chief of the Polish Army. He faced huge difficulties in what was still a largely rural country, and where living conditions varied widely between regions. Pilsudski's methods of forging a new Poland were often brutal, particularly towards minorities and his political opponents. Yet, in spite of many problems, there were notable achievements in the inter-war period including the establishment of social security and a state education system.

The Poles who came to Britain were born into this infant republic. Their backgrounds ranged from affluent lifestyles in cities such as Warsaw, Krakow, Lwow or Wilno, to subsistence living in poor farming areas. Whatever their aspirations for the future, most expected to be able to pursue them in an independent Poland. But in 1939 Poland was plunged into another period of partition, divided by Nazi Germany and the Soviet Union.

By the time peace was restored six years later, one in five citizens of pre-war Poland had been killed.

The Polish army had been the first to fight against Hitler, Britain had gone to war in defence of Poland's independence, and Polish servicemen had fought to defend Britain. Yet Poland was unrepresented at the Tehran and Yalta conferences where the British, Americans and Russians decided the fate of post-war Europe. The borders of Poland were moved again, two hundred miles to the west. The majority of Poles who were to settle in Britain found their homeland quite literally no longer existed. Nearly half of pre-war Poland was annexed by the Soviet Union. To 'compensate', land was taken from defeated Germany and made part of Poland, ruled over by a Communist regime controlled by Moscow. For Poles displaced by the War a return to life under the rule of Stalin was both unacceptable and dangerous. Their lives in exile had begun.

Members of the Polish Scouting Association at the outbreak of the War. They provided support to the army during the 1939 campaign, and were very active in the underground Home Army during the remainder of the War.

Sikorski Museum.

THE SECOND WORLD WAR

The Polish community in Britain settled here as a direct result of the Second World War. Their experiences during and after the War have shaped their concerns and politics ever since. The impact of the conflict on individuals has been deep and lasting, and as a result of it over a hundred thousand Poles in Britain spent a lifetime away from their families and homeland.

The Second World War began on 1st September 1939 when German troops poured across the Polish border. German air raids targeted the country's infrastructure, population, and especially its air force. Although outnumbered and ill-equipped, the Polish military defended their country courageously. It should have been an easy victory for the Germans, but it was not. They were surprised by the Poles' ability to keep fighting and regrouping in spite of bombardment from the air and rapid attacks on the ground. The fate of Poland was sealed on 17th September. As the result of a secret pre-War non-aggression pact between Nazi Germany and the Soviet Union, the Red Army entered Poland across the eastern border which was virtually unprotected. They met with little resistance, and by the beginning of October the last Polish garrisons had surrendered.

Despite the defeat of their armies and the occupation of Poland, an armistice was rejected by those military and political leaders who had escaped abroad. Contrary to declarations by the Germans and the Russians, Poland had not ceased to exist, and it would not cease to fight. The armed struggle now became the responsibility of the underground Home Army in Poland and of the many combatants who had escaped abroad. During the first month of the War Polish forces lost 66,000 men, 140,000 were wounded, and civilian casualties numbered many more. Their French and British allies, who the Poles understood were to come to their aid, were yet to fire a shot.

German and Soviet leaders divided Poland between them, fixing a demarcation line along the rivers Bug and San. In both occupied zones the regimes were brutal. Soviet oil fuelled the German military machine, and the propaganda of each commended the achievements of the other.

As the War continued the situation in Europe became increasingly chaotic. Accounts of British Poles' wartime experiences have been organised into the three general sections: those who escaped westwards in the early part of the War; those who spent the early part of the War under Soviet occupation; and those who lived in Nazi-occupied Poland.

People flee their bombed homes during the German invasion of western Poland. While the Polish forces lost 60,000 men killed, and 140,000 wounded, civilian casualties numbered many more.

Sikorski Museum.

"Through all that German occupation I lived in Kielce... German soldiers were taking people from the street, they needed people to work in Germany, to work in agriculture, in factories... We lived in an apartment on the high street and suddenly they said, 'They are coming, they are coming,' from door to door with sticks to hit people. What to do, how to hide? You can't go under the bed because they are slashing through the beds, or through the cupboard, in case somebody is hidden there."

German soldiers burning villages in western Poland. Equipped with 2,600 tanks against the Poles' 150, 2,000 war-planes against 400, the Germans waged a war against an enemy unable to reply in kind.

BHRU.

"Somebody told them this village provides us Partisans with food, bread, things like that... Germans took these photographs and took them to a Polish shop to be developed. One set was developed for them, and one set was developed for Polish Underground. Look how happy their faces are as they burn and kill people. I forgive always my enemy, but forget, no, I never."

"World War Two was a cataclysmic event, because it's what actually sparked off this enormous diaspora of Polish people. It had a huge effect on Polish people, partly because twenty percent of the Polish population died during World War Two, and that meant that every single family lost somebody, usually in appalling circumstances, so no family was left untouched. And secondly, this very large number of people left Poland and then couldn't return because of changed political circumstances. So it is a pivotal moment in time, because of that extraordinary loss of life and because of that very enforced, sudden diaspora of people."

Polish troops captured by the German army sit in the square of a town in southern Poland.

IWM.

"At that time, if Polish soldiers needed something, you just took it from the peasant. We say 'Right, horse and cart, now'. He had to give it. War is on. So we went, a huge column. I don't know how many because I can't see the front. And on these carts they put everything: telephone cables, clothes, some ammunition, things like that. And that column go towards Hungary."

"I was a regular army officer when War broke out and of course I took part in the campaign. We were not very successful because technically we were far inferior to the Germans, their equipment was far better. Nevertheless, we put up a good fight. We were fighting and retreating and finally I found myself in south-east Poland where the front line stabilised. We thought that probably our luck had changed, we had repulsed the Germans successfully. In fact, our hopes were shattered because we realised that we were attacked by Russians at the back."

During the Soviet invasion of eastern Poland 'Political Worker' Gilmanov talks to peasants in the village of Dubovitsi in Byelorussia. Against a background of mass arrests an election was held in which it was claimed that a huge majority had voted to make eastern Poland part of the Soviet Union.

IWM.

"After the Russians came it was very quiet and nobody knew what's going on. They stopped us singing Polish national anthem and we had to learn Russian anthem straight away. We couldn't move freely. In offices they were throwing out Polish people and putting in their people. We were sort of hanging in the air, we didn't know where we belonged. Everybody was frightened, nobody knew what's going on."

"There was a driver where I used to work who used to take the Russians around. He was very good at the Russian language and one day he says to me, 'You'd better get out of here because I've heard them, they want you to go to Russia because they want some skilled men there'. They asked me but I refused to go, then they told me they were taking me. There was a Polish group which used to go with a guide at night over the border into Hungary. I joined them."

"In their hearts the Poles refused to admit that the war was over. True, regular fighting on Polish soil came to an end, but it continued underground, it went on in foreign lands, by the side of Poland's allies."

When France was defeated in May 1940, 20,000 Polish soldiers escaped and made their way across the channel to Britain on Royal Navy and Polish ships.

Janina Struk.

ESCAPE TO THE WEST

With all of Poland under the control of the occupying armies by the end of September 1939, the Polish government fled south to Romania, where they were interned. Due to German and Soviet pressure, Polish troops who had escaped to Romania and Hungary in large numbers were also interned. The French government offered to receive these troops, but with the leadership locked up the task of moving them was not easy. The evacuation to France took nine months, with men also transferred to Yugoslavia and Italy.

The Polish government then mandated its powers to a group of Polish leaders at liberty in France. General Sikorski became Prime Minister, and as Commander-in-Chief, was charged with raising a new army. Throughout Poland's past struggles to regain independence Polish armies had often been formed abroad, and so this move was founded on a sound practical and historical basis. However the shortage of available men in France was the first symptom of a problem that was to recur throughout the War: Poland could not match the manpower and resources of her allies and thus maintain her interests on an equal footing. General Sikorski had to draw on those soldiers who had escaped from Poland, refugees, and Poles already living in France. Although the French government pledged money and equipment, they were initially loathe to release the many Polish immigrants working in France's coal mines. Eventually an agreement was reached, and by the time Hitler invaded France in the spring of 1940 there were 80,000 Polish troops in France, with others stationed in the Middle East and Scandinavia.

The German advance through France was rapid and by 14th June they had occupied Paris. Three days later the French government asked for a ceasefire. This was a disaster for the Polish cause. Their best military units had suffered badly defending France and were now dispersed or had crossed into neutral Switzerland. Many of those who had been recruited locally simply joined French soldiers in going home again. However the Polish government-in-exile announced their intention to fight on and moved to London where they remained for the duration of the War. Their main aims were to rebuild the Polish Armed Forces abroad, to control and aid the resistance movement (the Home Army) in Poland, and to conduct diplomatic relationships overseas. Those military units still intact were evacuated from France to British ports on Royal Navy and Polish vessels. The first Poles to arrive in Britain had been sailors, the majority of the Polish Merchant Marine fleet and Navy having made remarkable escapes to Britain shortly after Germany's attack on Poland. Some army units had also escaped to Palestine, a British-controlled territory in the Middle East. From here they went into action in North Africa, most notably at Tobruk, and later fought in Italy.

With the remains of Britain's own army desperately regrouping in the south of England it was decided to send the 20,000 Polish troops who had arrived to Scotland, where they could reorganise and train. The War Office requisitioned parts of Lanarkshire, and large tented camps were set up around the towns of Douglas, Crawford and Biggar, with men also billeted in schools and with local people. Ironically as Scotland welcomed the Polish troops, many of their own soldiers captured in France were being interned in German prisoner-of-war camps in occupied Poland. Several were to escape and join Poland's Home Army.

With the threat of a German invasion imminent the Polish troops were initially assigned to the defence of Scotland's eastern coastline. Although they were placed under British operational command, like their compatriots in the Polish Navy and Air Force they were responsible to the Polish Government and had a fair degree of autonomy. In all three cases they made up the largest foreign contingent serving with the British forces. During 1940 the War must have seemed more remote to the army than to those members of the Polish Air Force who had been reunited at airbases throughout England. They played a pivotal role in the airborne Battle of Britain which unfolded during the autumn, Polish fighter

At the outbreak of War both the Polish Navy and the merchant fleet sought sanctuary in British ports, and were later to play an important role in keeping supply routes to Britain open.

IWM.

"Going out on the convoys, most of the time it was very boring, but dangerous because the Germans were sending out U-boats and battleships. In 1941 we were returning from Canada, and we met The Bismark, a big battleship! After it had sunk the British cruiser the H.M.S. Hood it tried to escape, the Royal Navy tried to catch it and we joined in. I remember seeing it at sunset, a fearsome sight!"

squadrons shooting down one in six of German planes destroyed. The British Secretary of State for the Air Force recorded that: 'Our shortage of trained pilots would have made it impossible to man the squadrons which were required to defeat the German air force and so win the Battle of Britain, if the gallant airmen of Poland had not leapt into the breach'. The Poles also formed their own bomber squadrons which took part in raids over occupied Europe during the course of the War.

As the conflict progressed the submarines and ships of the Polish Navy were involved in keeping the supply routes open across the Atlantic and Arctic, as well as fighting in Norway and the Mediterranean. In Scotland the continued presence of the army brought Poles into almost every community in Fife, Perthshire, Forfar and Angus. As well as military duties the men helped with agricultural work on farms short of labour. As their army developed, Polish regiments were presented with standards or trumpet banners from Scottish towns and cities. They returned the honour by incorporating various Scottish emblems, such as thistles or lions rampant, into their badges.

There were also more personal relationships, the spirit of a shared cause and the famous charm and elegant manners of the Poles winning them friends. Liaisons, engagements, and marriages with local women became commonplace, despite the need to overcome a number of problems, not least that of language. It was not unusual for newly married women to have trouble pronouncing their own surname. By marrying a foreigner, these women automatically lost their British citizenship and until 1946, as aliens in their own country, they had to report regularly to the local police station. Many couples also had to surmount a degree of prejudice from the local community. It was one thing to have your 'gallant allies' living in your midst, but quite another if they were to marry your daughter or your sister. As the Poles were almost exclusively Roman Catholic there was also a degree of religious bigotry to be endured. However some organisations, such as the British Council, set about promoting links. Language classes were organised in both English and Polish, and clubs and canteens set up for off-duty soldiers. Exhibitions, dances and concerts featuring artists and musicians serving in the Polish forces were advertised in newspapers and magazines established to serve this new emigre community.

In building up their forces, the Polish Command concentrated on two key areas. Their experience of German blitzkrieg convinced them of the importance of armoured formations, and as a result tanks of the 1st Polish Armoured Division became a common sight, training alongside the infantry formations. It was also decided to form an airborne brigade, which could be dropped into occupied Poland to assist the resistance movement in a future uprising against the occupying Germans. However relations with their allies were becoming strained. In November 1943 when the British, American and Soviet leaders met in Tehran, Poland was unrepresented. It was secretly decided to move the post-war Polish state westwards. The Soviet Union would absorb territory in the east, and Poland would take over German territory to the west. When later put to the Polish government in London they, and the Home Army command in Warsaw, were adamant. A surrender of land to Russia, particularly one which included the cities of Lwow and Wilno, would mean that Poland would become a Soviet puppet, and 'compensation' elsewhere was irrelevant.

However the plans of the 'Big Three' were to prevail. For many Poles in Britain, they meant that to see their homes again after the War, they would have to become Soviet citizens. As Polish soldiers became aware of this, there were great feelings of bitterness and betrayal. However they remained loyal to their alliance. On the day that the Home Army rose up in Warsaw, 1st August 1944, Polish men of the 1st Armoured Division landed in France to join the invasion forces. After inflicting a crucial defeat on the Germans at Falaise, they helped liberate Belgium and the Netherlands, and reached Wilhelmshaven naval base in northern Germany by the end of the War. Meanwhile the Polish paratroopers, given the choice, would have preferred to be fighting in Warsaw. Instead they found themselves involved in the ill-fated operation at Arnhem, part of an unsuccessful plan to capture fiercely defended bridges across which the Allies could advance into Germany. They were then withdrawn to Britain for reorganisation, and the final surrender of Germany in May 1945 came before they saw active service again.

When Polish forces fled their occupied homeland they made their way firstly to France to regroup, and after France's defeat in 1940, on to Britain. Many were interned in countries through which they passed, such as these prisoners in Spain.

Sikorski Museum.

"We'd been fighting in Poland for nearly three weeks and the Germans were pushing us back. We were told 'We're going to counterattack,' so all the reserves went to the east of Poland to make a counterattack against the Germans. But as soon as we got there the Russians entered. We were lucky because we escaped on vehicles to Romania. Those who were walking, Russians took them to Siberia. At the Romanian border, we had to throw our guns in a pile. One officer shot himself, he was so proud, he wouldn't give in. In the Romanian camps we slept on straw, no beds, just straw. We had our own blankets. Food was mostly tea and dry bread, no butter. Dinner time there was sort of soup, but it was mostly water. Anyway it didn't kill us. But Romanian soldiers, they were a poor lot. They didn't have shoes, just part of a tyre tied to their feet with string, and their rifle had string for a strap."

Prime Minister Sikorski and the Polish government-in-exile meeting in London, which became the focus of Polish hopes for liberation throughout the War.

IWM.

"The aims of the government-in-exile were to work for independence, work for truth over the Katyn massacre, to help the people of Poland and keep Polish people informed via Radio Free Europe and the BBC."

"We stayed under Soviet occupation for a fortnight. We knew our days would be numbered, being members of the Polish 'fascist' army we shall be deported to Siberia, done away with. So we decided to walk over the Carpathian mountains to Hungary. We walked for ten nights, night-time only because Soviet forces were all over. We were lucky. And then, after a fortnight, the two of us left Hungary and travelled through Yugoslavia and Italy and came to France. I joined the French Polish soldiers. When France collapsed I got to the English channel, and two merchant boats picked up about a thousand of us or so. Squished into those two boats it took us three days to get to Liverpool. Later the British government approached the Polish government in London and said 'We can employ three or four hundred of your officers in West Africa'. A few of us volunteered. Adventure, romantic, beautiful, I thought. And I landed in Sierra Leone, only later on I learned the original name 'White Man's Grave'. Every one of us developed malaria. We were deployed there to train the forces."

On arrival in Britain the vast majority of Polish troops were billeted in Scotland where they underwent further training and were allocated coastal defence duties.

Sikorski Museum.

"We arrived from France and there were buses waiting for us. And we came to Eastchurch RAF camp [Kent]. Beautiful beds, clean sheets, nice polished floor, everything. And straight away they took us for a medical. We had a bath and they gave us new clothes, uniform of course. We went to have tea and I remember those big tea urns, we had to put cups underneath and the tea was sweet. And after that tea we could have jam on bread. I said 'Is it always like this?'. 'Oh yes, always like this.' This is how we found England. Nice, nice place."

Polish soldiers at a training camp in Scotland. Although they were armed and commanded by the British throughout the War, Polish units retained a large degree of independence.

Sikorski Museum.

"In 1940 we were taken to Crawford [South Lanarkshire]. We were under canvas, and if the rain comes and you touch the canvas, you flood it, they're not waterproof. Then we move to Blairgowrie, not very far from Perth. Most of the soldiers were sleeping in the town hall, and my platoon had the church hall, so we were comfortable. We stayed there for about a year-and-a-half."

Off duty Polish soldiers and local women in Scotland. Although a few dependents came with the armed forces the wartime Polish community was mostly a male one.

Sikorski Museum.

"I met my wife in Scotland. That was a good time, going to dances. Actually she was a girlfriend of a Scottish boy, and she dropped him and came to me. All the English I knew was 'I go, you go, bus go, Glasgow,' that's all I knew."

"When we were in uniform there were always arguments between ourselves and English people, English lads especially, because we were for the lasses, you know. We could always get a partner on the dance floor or a chat in a pub, because we had a different approach to women, you see. We brought it from home that the woman is to be respected and put on a pedestal. You would go and kiss her on the hand, and even curtsey to her. Some of them didn't even know that such a thing could exist. I can see I've changed myself now, and I don't kiss anybody's hand, but in those days it was a very important thing."

Polish Air Force units were reunited in Britain and expanded with new recruits. Here they undergo a training flight over Scotland in 1940.

IWM.

"I treated my flying in the Airforce as my duty and as a pleasure. I could express myself. I don't think I ever overdid it, but to some people it might seem that way... My wife was in the booking office in the railway station at Chesterfield and I was flying at Hucknall outside Nottingham. Only a few minutes and I was in Chesterfield... And I didn't overdo it, just dive over the station, do a victory roll and a loop, then done..."

"I was posted to the 304 Polish squadron patrolling over the sea, escorting convoys. We had a radar with which we could discover submarines. I was sent to Cranwell flying school where I studied radar. We were not allowed a notebook with us, everything we learned was memory. We'd to be very secretive about it. Because the English trusted the Poles we were the first foreign unit to be let into the secret of the radar."

Reloading a Hurricane aircraft with ammunition. The Polish Air Force numbered over 14,000 men by the end of the war, and played a huge role in the Battle of Britain and flying missions over occupied Europe.

IWM.

"We set off for Hanover, about twelve aeroplanes. As soon as we entered the North Sea, the Germans were at us and planes were coming down in flames... When we came over our target you could see exactly what was happening, there was such a fire on the ground, and all the search lights. Crews were bailing out and planes were being shot down. One of our planes was carrying three one-thousand-pound bombs and he was only about fifty yards from us. Just before he reached his target he was blown up, there was no sign of a plane left, they were gone completely from the air."

"They sent me to the RAF station at Newton to train for an operation to Poland... But before we set off I had to go to a doctor for medical clearance. I said, 'Doctor, please check my ears, otherwise I'm ok'. My ears were completely wet, running and itching. So he says, 'Sorry but I cannot sign the certificate, I have to send you to hospital'. Somehow they found a spare wireless operator and my crew went to Poland without me. But on the way back the pilot made a forced landing in the sea, short of petrol. Four members of the crew got drowned... I would have been on that mission."

In 1943 the Poles were dealt a devastating blow when their wartime leader, General Sikorski, was killed in a plane crash in Gibraltar. This picture shows his funeral cortège passing through Newark where he was buried.

Sikorski Museum.

"Sikorski had great personal integrity, and his death was a personal tragedy. It also lessened the chances of gaining an independent Poland. Britain and Russia were clearly in dialogue about the way Europe was to be carved up. Poland was on the fracture line, but historically saw itself allied with the West. Sikorski's death left a vacuum. He was respected, and a very hard act to follow. From very early on there was a view that there was a conspiracy, people considered his death may well have been deliberate."

A Dutch civilian moves his belongings past tanks of the Polish First Armoured Division sheltering beneath a windmill outside Breda in Holland.

Sikorski Museum.

"Everybody in the Parachute Brigade was dreaming we would be the first to be dropped into Poland. But things changed. Towards the end of the War things were not looking bright for us. Our country was being sold to the Russians, but our honour meant we would carry on fighting."

Polish army units made a notable contribution to the Allied invasion and campaign in occupied Europe. These men are entering Breda in Holland after its liberation by Polish troops.

Sikorski Museum.

"My father always remembers his forces days as being the absolute happiest time of his life. Although the War was traumatic and disruptive, he actually found the companionship and the work that people did together a very happy time personally. For him, he captured more of the thing that one sometimes hears about from other people, about wartime pulling people together, and actually having fun in adversity, being in that sort of sociable situation. Whereas I don't think my mother would ever see the War in those terms."

Farming family in south-east Poland, 1936.

IACRC.

DEPORTATION TO THE EAST

On 17th September 1939, the Soviet Union invaded Poland from the east. With the Polish armed forces fully committed to fighting the Germans, the Red Army advance was virtually unopposed, and the defeat of Poland was inevitable. 200,000 Polish troops were taken prisoner by the Red Army. The secret pre-war pact between Hitler and Stalin meant that Poland was divided once more.

The Communists confiscated land and property, nationalised industry and banks and collectivised agriculture. The 'racial enemies' of the Nazis were mirrored in the 'class enemies' of the Soviet system. Stalin set out to solve forever what he considered to be the problem of the Polish nation by attempting to obliterate it both culturally and physically. The Soviet secret police, the NKVD, were even more destructive during the early part of the War than their German counterparts. They had refined the techniques of political terror in previous collectivisation campaigns and purges in other parts of the Soviet Union. Polish leaders were targeted in an immediate wave of arrests and deportations. People were classified and segregated. Rigged elections in November 1939 installed governing assemblies of Ukrainians and Byelorussians. A referendum was held and it was claimed that 92% of the population wanted the newly-occupied territories to become part of the Soviet Union.

Later that winter the brutal deportation of over one-and-a-half million Polish citizens began. They were taken to camps near the Arctic circle, in the far east of the Soviet Union, and in the central Asian republics of Kazakhstan and Uzbekistan. Those people identified as being influential, such as professionals, government employees, and members of the clergy were particular targets; but as long as deportees were Polish, few distinctions were made. Farmers, bankers, students, railway workers, professors - people from all walks of life - were taken with their entire families in four vast railway convoys that left in February, April, and June 1940, and in June 1941. Communities were rounded up at night by the NKVD and taken to rail depots. When enough people had been gathered, they were packed into unheated and windowless cattle-wagons for rail journeys of up to six thousand miles, sometimes lasting over a month. Food supplies were meagre and starvation, frostbite, disease, derangement and infanticide claimed a huge toll. Corpses had to be pushed through a hole in the floor or the wall which also served as a toilet. Once unloaded from the trains, many faced further journeys in the holds of riverboats or on the backs of lorries, as they were dispersed to the most remote recesses of the Soviet Union. Once at their destination, large numbers continued to die through lack of food, disease, or exhaustion. They worked in appalling conditions as slave labourers in mines, cutting timber, building roads or digging canals. Regimes at the camps were controlled by the NKVD and were often brutal, designed to extract the maximum amount of work from each person. Those unable to work due to infancy, old age, illness or infirmity were often denied food rations.

In June 1941 Hitler's armies invaded the Soviet Union and the 'eternal friendship' between the Germans and the Russians was over. Had it continued for much longer it is doubtful that the Polish nation could have survived. In 1941 the Nazi extermination machine was moving into top gear, and was matched in its brutality by the Soviets. However Hitler's invasion of the Soviet Union turned Russia from an accomplice in genocide to an uneasy ally of Poland, and as the War progressed the Germans proved unable to destroy Poland on their own. Almost half of the Poles deported to Soviet slave labour camps were already dead. After difficult negotiations between Stalin and the Polish government-in-exile in London, the survivors were offered an 'amnesty'. A Polish army was created in the Soviet Union under the leadership of General Anders, a military commander who had himself spent the previous two years in Moscow's notorious Lubianka prison. Although the Soviets welcomed the

Belomor slave labour camp. 100,000 died, many of them Polish, in the construction of the canal at Belomor on the White Sea, near the Russian Arctic Circle.

David King.

"10th February, 1940, in the morning, about six or seven o'clock. A bang on the door. The militia walked in and they said to father, 'Hands up, stand in the corner'. They said to mother, 'You pack what you can manage but don't pack much because you have to walk to the railway station'. So you can imagine, what could we take? Mother put a lot of clothes on us, we could hardly walk... It was such a severe winter and there was a long, long train... for taking cows. They weren't for humans, and they packed us in. There was about fifty in one carriage, can you imagine? They locked the door, the window was covered with white ice. We couldn't see anything but I could hear whispers... our neighbours and aunts and uncles. And I could hear our dog. He was running right from our home, twenty kilometres to the station. You should have heard those dogs. Everybody thought it was the end of the world."

extra troops to fight the Germans, they were reluctant to lose the slave labour that helped to fuel their war. News of the 'amnesty' filtered through to the labour camps fitfully, and little help was offered to enable people to leave places in the middle of the wilderness. Around 160,500 Poles did finally manage to escape, but 881,000 remained, some to this day.

Assembly points in Russia were agreed for the organisation and training of this new army. However food, clothing and equipment promised by the Soviets failed to materialise and with the onset of winter it was decided to move the 44,000 starving and sick men who had gathered further south. Their new headquarters were near Tashkent in Uzbekistan. Reception camps were set up in Soviet Central Asia, and for the first time civilian refugees camped alongside the soldiers. The refugees had made arduous and miserable journeys. Hungry, homeless and harassed by the NKVD, they had often waited weeks for documents or transport. Although they had escaped the cold, diseases such as typhus and dysentery thrived in the warmer climate of the camps. At the height of the epidemics Polish Army doctors estimated that one in two were infected with contagious disease. The outcome was - once again - death on a vast scale.

By March 1942 Stalin finally conceded that the Soviets were no longer able to provide sufficient food for the Polish army and gave permission for them and the civilians to be evacuated to areas of the Middle East under British control. In Iran 'Anders' Army' as they had become known, were received by the Polish Brigade of Carpathian Riflemen, assembled from soldiers who had escaped from France, Hungary and Romania earlier during the War. Any able-bodied civilians of military age were transferred to military units, and transport organised to take remaining refugees to safer areas. The majority went to camps in British India and East Africa. Some camps were small temporary affairs, others were large and allowed Polish culture and language to flourish. For example the camp at Valivade, near Goa in Southern India, was built to accommodate 5,000 and had its own church, theatre, and shops. Its nine schools had a total of 3,250 pupils, and in the orphanage were 400 children.

Meanwhile the military personnel were undergoing intensive training in the Middle East and the newly created Polish Second Corps were assigned to the British Eighth Army, with General Anders keeping overall command. The Polish Women's Auxiliary Service worked as ferry pilots, in offices, hospitals, transport, and canteens, and organised multitudes of orphans. Many women also travelled to Britain to provide similar services, and a few flew transport planes in the Polish Air Force. Teenagers were brought to Britain for military training.

By early 1944 the Second Corps had transferred to Italy to join the Allies fighting their way northwards. The turning point of the Italian campaign came in May when the Second Corps were assigned to break the five month German defence of Monte Cassino. After this famous victory further successes culminated in the Polish forces liberating Bologna in northern Italy, one week before the final German capitulation in the country.

However any sense of victory Poles felt at the end of the War was negated by despair at the fate of Poland. An earlier plan for the Second Corps to play an active role in the liberation of Poland had come to nothing, and their country was now occupied by the Red Army. Their feelings were crystallised by the Katyn affair, which remains a source of intense anger and betrayal even today. After the 'amnesty' of 1941, it became clear that 15,000 Polish army officers had simply disappeared after their detention in 1939. Most were not professional soldiers but reservists mobilised at the outbreak of war. They were well-trained graduates - teachers, businessmen, doctors and scientists - and in the eyes of the Soviets **the** class enemy. In 1943 thousands of corpses, each with a bullet in the back of the head, were discovered by the advancing Germans in the Katyn forest near Smolensk in Russia. Although the Soviets denied responsibility, the evidence was overwhelming. Fearful of upsetting Stalin, the British ignored the Katyn affair. Churchill dismissed it with a terse 'There is no use prowling around the three-year-old graves of Smolensk'. For the Poles it became the symbol both of their betrayal by the Allies, and of countless other atrocities committed by the Soviet Union against the Polish nation.

Polish soldiers captured by the Soviet army were the first to be deported to the wildernesses of Siberia in the winter of 1939/40, and had to construct their own labour camps, often while sheltering in holes dug in the snow. This is a typical bunker dug into the earth where people lived.

BHRU.

"We were loaded on horse-driven sledges, because nothing else would get through, and about two hours later we were loaded on cattle wagons. All the way it was about 5,000 miles - a month on a train. Until we reached Moscow we were left in our own filth, but once past Moscow we were allowed to go out to the toilet, although there were army blokes marching round the train all the time."

"We were herded into cattle wagons for transportation. The trucks were dark and locked, there was only one small window at the top. 'Bunks' had been made, planks of wood on the side of the wagon. Cramming in as many individuals as they could, we stood during the day and slept of a fashion at night. We were given no food at all for the first two days. We were expected to eat anything we had brought with us. People were distressed and crying. One woman gave birth to a stillborn child, the guards threw the body off the train when we reached a station. You had to try not to touch the wooden walls when you slept, your hair would stick to the wood because of the ice and break off. It was bitterly cold."

Polish deportees cutting timber in a Siberian labour camp in the summer of 1940. The man second from right eventually found himself serving with the Polish Parachute Brigade, based in Scotland, and after the War settled in Fife.

National Museums of Scotland.

"The weather was continuously freezing cold. You were lucky if you had your own blanket as no bedding was issued. I was very lucky as I still had my pillow with me. Those who survived were set to work in the forest, felling the trees. The men cut the trees down and the women and older children sorted the wood into sizes. My husband and I worked as part of a team of four people, from 6am in the morning until 6pm at night, in extremely deep snow, up to my chest. It was exhausting work. When we were in the depths of the forest chopping wood, we would take a piece of bread to eat with us as a meal. By the time it came to eating it, the bread was frozen solid and we had to thaw it out over bits of burning wood. It was bitterly cold and dark, like a deep freeze. If you cried your tears would freeze on to your cheeks. If you kept your eyes closed from the wind your eyelids would stick together. My husband, some of his family, and I, lived like this for two years. We all looked like skin and bones, everyone in the camp was so thin. The snow began melting half-way through June. There were almost two months of a Siberian summer when forest flowers grew and bloomed incredibly quickly. There were plenty of tiny wild flowers, the only bright colours around."

Many Polish workers were taken to the cotton growing areas of Kazakhstan, as seen here, and Uzbekistan. Much of the labour used in these Soviet Republics of Central Asia was that of women and children, who were made to dig irrigation canals.

Sikorski Museum.

"I worked for about two months on the Steppes, with a Kazak family. I was the only European there. They had a baby, and we had just one big kettle for everything. She used to cook in it, she used to bath the baby in it, she used to do the nappies in it, everything."

"Conditions... oh it was shocking because there were big, very long, timber-built huts. And there were about three iron-built stoves in the middle for heating. We burned wood in them. They were riddled with cockroaches, and the bed bugs were absolutely terrible. After a time we stretched cords across, and hung up blankets to make it more private. Each family was separated by blankets."

It is estimated that of those deported from Poland 380,000 were children. Together with the elderly they were particularly vulnerable to starvation and disease. Typhus and dysentery in particular were common throughout the settlements.

Sikorski Museum.

"We all were same age, twelve years old, and we had to load heavy pieces of wood for so many hours a day, in the cold, without proper food. Then we put them into an oven to dry, and as they came out we had to take a hack-saw and slice them. And I worked so hard but my father had to pay for my food because I couldn't make the target. Well they called it food. It wasn't, it was water and bread, that's all. Only on national days, the first and second of May, the Socialist big days, we were allowed about a quarter pound of sweets and a double portion of bread and coffee... I was so weak I could hardly stand on my legs."

"Me, as a young girl, they wanted to send me to school, but my parents wouldn't agree, which I don't know whether was right or wrong. They thought I would be brought up as a Communist and probably they would never see me again... I think they did right, but I had to go to work."

"Only kind of meat we got was when a horse died, when it had to be destroyed. I was working with a horse. We used to drag trunks from the forest to the saw-mills... We were short of vitamins and everything. A lot of people were losing their sight at evening time. Even when it was light, you could only see like you were in a fog... We used to follow the horses, they took us back to the place where we were living."

General Sikorski inspecting troops with General Anders at Buzuluk, the assembly point in Russia for men just released from the camps as a result of the German invasion of the Soviet Union. General Anders had just been appointed leader of this new army, the Polish Second Corps.

IWM.

"Germany invaded Russia and we didn't know what was going on. They told us to gather - Polish people only...They told us, 'You are free people because we want you to help us fight the Germans'."

"It was Churchill who made the agreement with Stalin that the Poles will be amnestied. We were furious about it, what amnesty? We didn't commit any crime."

"General Anders was like Moses to us because he led us from Russia into the free world."

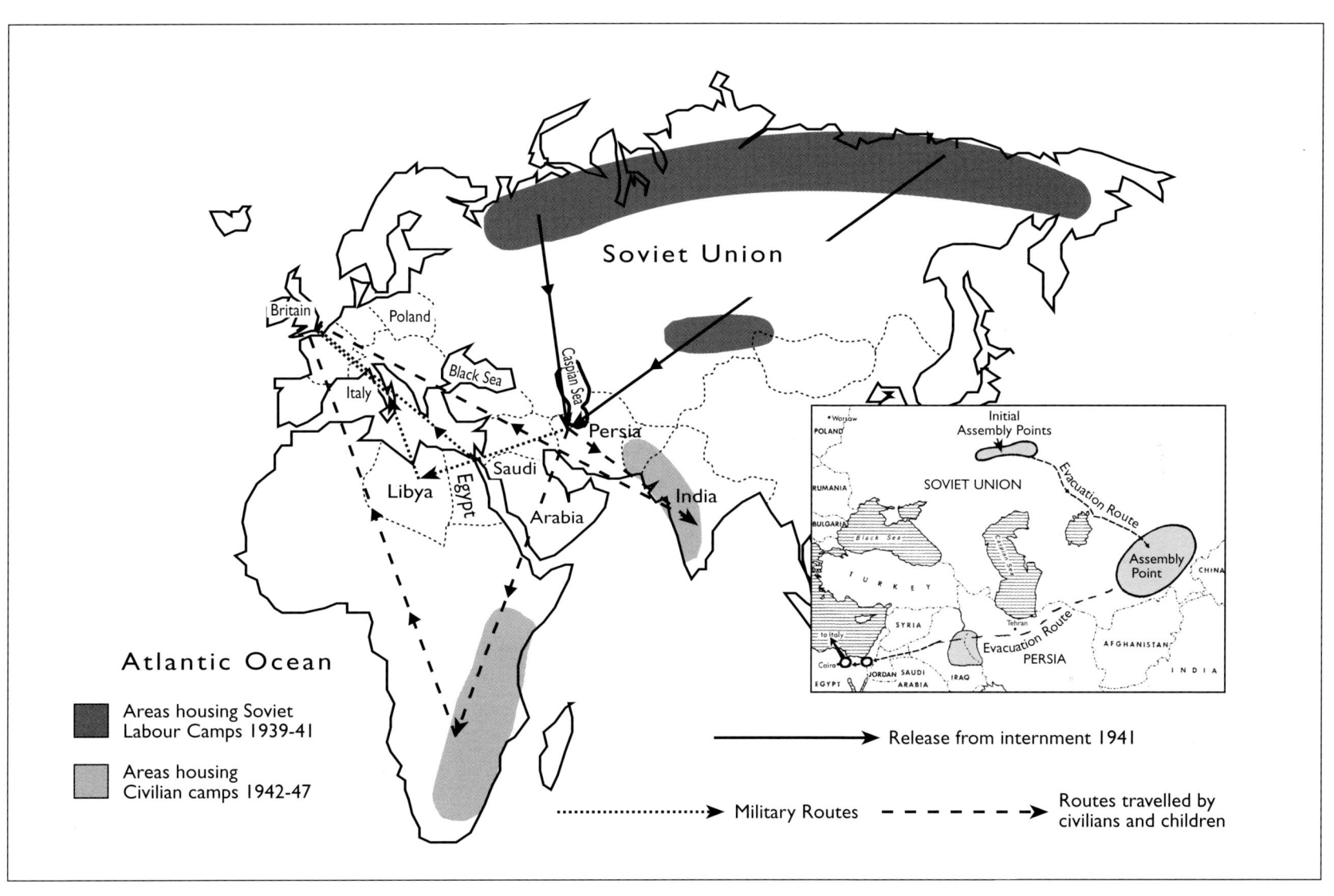

Routes taken from Stalin's labour camps to Britain after the 'amnesty' of 1941.

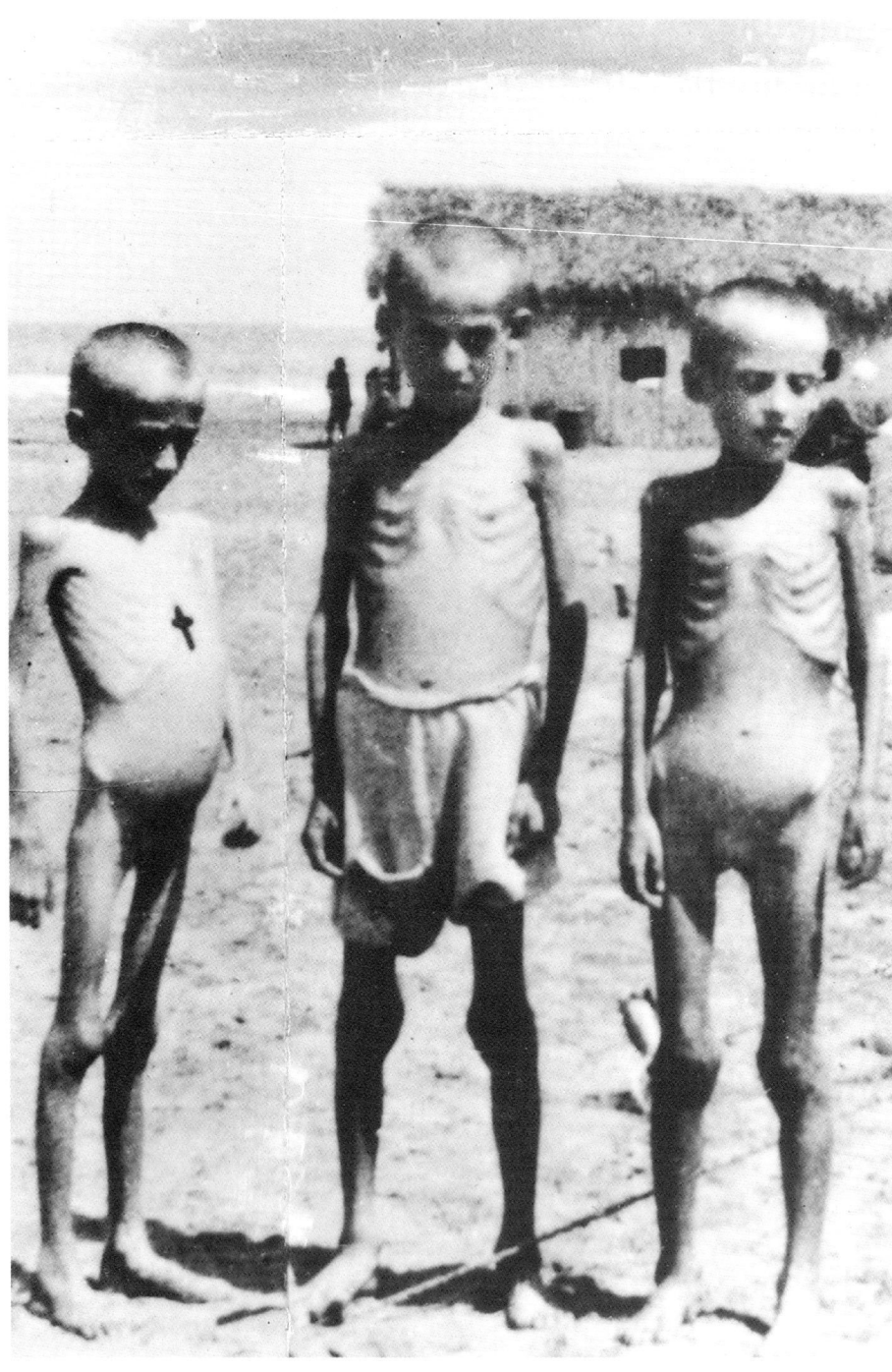

Children making their way to reception camps in the Middle East after their escape from the Soviet Union.

Sikorski Museum.

"We started to travel, but we had no food, and if you had no food you would die during the journey. There was no way to survive because they didn't give you even a piece of bread. Was dreadful conditions, dreadful. People falling down and nobody cared, because of hunger. And then... typhoid, dysentery, you've never seen anything like it. People were dying like flies. Travelling by train, there was no water, so we managed to put a string on a little bucket to catch snow. We walked on dead people, believe me."

"In a town where the train stopped, my father and myself went out to try to buy something. We still had some gold, a few things, mama's necklace and clock. So of course, you could sell it and buy something from the Uzbeks. Father managed to buy soup to bring to the transport that was waiting for us. But my father dropped it. He had a severe heart attack... people behind us ran quickly, 'What's happened?' and they called the militia. They said 'He's dead... if you want to see where your father's going to be taken you can go with us'. They took us in a little car and we came to a huge building. As they opened the gate all I could see were bodies of dead people, and they just took my father's arms and legs and swing him right to the top, shut the gate, and that's it."

Due to the appalling conditions, and well-founded distrust of Stalin, it was decided to evacuate Polish troops and civilians to British-occupied areas of the Middle East. Here civilians are seen arriving at a camp in Tehran.

Sikorski Museum.

"In Uzbekistan there was a place where they were collecting soldiers, so Stan, my brother, went to the army and I stayed in a little village. Huts were just made of clay, a bit of straw, and lice. We found a lady, she was so badly bitten by lice and everything, she wasn't able to help herself. She must have had TB, and in three or four days she died. We had to report it and they came and took the body away. We chucked everything out because we were afraid of lice, if they bit you, you might catch typhoid. They cut all our hair off and took our clothes because of the lice. About six weeks later we left for Iran."

Those arriving in the Middle East were already exhausted by their journeys, and weak from hunger and disease. The warmer climate encouraged epidemics such as typhus and dysentery. Hospital camps, such as this one in Persia [see map], were full and death rates were high.

Sikorski Museum.

"When we got to Iran there was thousands of tents on the sand, near the Caspian Sea, and they kept us there. Of course, they took everything off us again, shaved and washed us to stop epidemics. And they gave us some food, but we had to be very careful because we were so hungry. A lot of people died because they didn't have food for a long time and they started eating, grabbing everything, and they had problems with their insides and died. You had to be very careful, eat small portions, avoid heavy things, and those who took no notice wouldn't survive. Even drinking water - just a sip and stop, then an hour later try again. I survived but lots of young people died in Iran."

A family is reunited in a camp for civilians near Tehran.

Sikorski Museum.

"In Iran... we hadn't much food, but enough to survive, and I began to become myself. But I had yellow jaundice, or something, so mum had a ring and she sold it because they told me to have plenty of fruit, but you had to buy it. I've always had problems with my liver and stomach and I think that's what caused it. I've never been right since."

Many of those who could not be recruited into the armed forces because of their age or health were made members of the Red Cross and then cared for the large numbers of civilian refugees.

BHRU.

"Initially my mother and her parents went to Tashkent in the south of Russia. Because my grandfather was a politician he was flown out from Tashkent and brought to England to participate in the Polish government. But my mother and her mother had to come out overland, and they assisted in bringing out a large group of children who had been orphaned in Siberia. They were brought out in a land convoy through Persia, where they stopped for six weeks for some emergency feeding, because the children were dreadfully malnourished. I have a photograph of my mother from that time where she is still terribly thin from her time in Siberia. Then they went to India where they set up an orphanage for these children and worked in the Red Cross. They spent about a year in India, and then got on a ship that was in a convoy and travelled to South Africa. They lived in Durban for nearly a year while waiting for availability on another convoy, and eventually managed to join my grandfather. My mother's first landing was the port of Greenock in Scotland, not a particularly scenic introduction. She thought it was fairly dismal to be perfectly honest."

The vast majority of civilians then travelled on to safer places further away from the fighting. Camps were set up throughout the British Empire, particularly in East Africa and India. This orphanage for Polish children was run by Polish Red Cross staff in Bombay.

BHRU.

"We took elderly people, women and children, and we were going to settle them away from the war front. Kids of seven, or that kind of age, were with us, on the way to Africa, and on the Indian Ocean we had a three-day storm. I was in charge of going to inspect all the people in the boat. There were no cabins for them, they were in the rooms below deck. I think it was about 8,000 people were together there, and I don't think there were two dozen who weren't sick. Oh terrible, so sick. There weren't any portholes so they couldn't be sick there so the smell was terrible. Couldn't eat or anything. And those children were in there."

Orphans aged between fifteen and seventeen who were flown to Britain from the Middle East begin their training as aircraft apprentices in the Technical Training Command of the Royal Air Force.

Sikorski Museum.

"The Prime Minister, General Sikorski, wanted some volunteers to join the Polish Air Force under the British command. And ever since I was a very young boy I always wanted to be a pilot... Oh, I thought, that's something for me."

Jadwiga Pilsudska, one of the women pilots who flew in the Polish Air Force.

Sikorski Museum.

"There were a few women pilots. They were transport flying, they used to bring new planes to England from Africa and Canada, various places. And they were very good pilots because they had to get used to all different kinds of aircraft. But they never did fly on operational missions. Jadwiga Pilsudska was the famous one, she was the daughter of Pilsudski, our past president."

"After France collapsed the Carpathian Brigade moved to Palestine because the British forces were there... a lot of Poles escaping from Hungary and Romania eventually met in Palestine... Eventually we had to defend Libya from Italy and General Rommel. There was a ding-dong battle for a month in the desert. Was like cat and mouse, who had more tanks had the advantage of it. In the meantime refugees came, the people who had been taken to labour camps in Russia. Those fit to join the forces joined there."

Graves of Polish soldiers killed while fighting as part of the British Eighth Army in North Africa.

Sikorski Museum.

Members of the Second Corps celebrating Soldiers Day, August 1942. Based mainly in Iraq the men who had left Russia in poor health were now undergoing intense training and on their way to becoming an army.

Sikorski Museum.

"After Palestine we went to Africa. It was a splendid life, plenty of food and everything. There was General Sikorski and the Polish government in London. We had powerful friends. Mr Churchill called us his 'dear Polish friends and heroes'. President Roosevelt called the Poles 'the inspiration of the world'. There was good news that the Polish Air Force was helping win the War. The Polish Navy was fighting alongside the British Navy so we were very happy. We were looking forward!"

Polish soldiers on leave in Luxor, Egypt, 1943. In September of this year the Allies invaded Italy, and the transfer of the Second Corps to Italy took place over the winter.

Sikorski Museum.

"I joined the army in Russia and later on we went to Iran. I spent four weeks near the Caspian Sea. The army I enjoyed very much because we saw many countries... We went to Iraq and I did a special course: how to speak English... I met my husband on this course, and later on we went to Egypt, Palestine, Italy. And look how many countries I saw!"

In May 1944 the turning point of the Italian campaign came with the Battle of Monte Cassino, a key route to Rome. Where previous assaults had failed, the Second Corps secured a famous victory, but with the loss of nearly 4,000 killed and wounded.

IWM.

"We went to Monte Cassino. They sent us to relieve Scottish troops... We went to this meeting and they showed us a plastic map, where Germans were and everything. Oh boy, goodness, when I come back I says to my mate, 'Have you got clean underwear, because you'll be lucky if you come out wounded from that place where we're going!'"

Aerial view of the hill top fortress of the monastery at Monte Cassino after its capture by Polish troops. From here the Second Corps continued to fight northwards as part of the Allied advance, and at the end of the War found itself in northern Italy.

IWM.

"Twelve hundred guns bashed for two hours before we went into action. The Germans started firing as we advanced. My wireless was flat, but my radio actually saved me. I put it in front of me and I lay down, but my mate got killed in an explosion. I was wounded and trying to speak but blood was coming from my mouth, radio was out of action, so I was useless. Air was like gunpowder, little bits of black... nothing left of trees, only sticks... I finished up in hospital, my mate got killed."

View of Warsaw at the end of the War. After the Warsaw Rising the entire civilian population was removed to internment camps. Hitler then ordered the complete razing of the city, so that no settlement would rise there ever again. By the time the demolition squads had finished, 93% of the city's buildings were destroyed.

BHRU.

LIFE UNDER THE NAZIS

The German conquest of Poland brought twenty-two million Polish citizens under the terror of Nazi rule, and Hitler set about his stated aim for Poland, that it was 'to be swept off the face of the earth'. Northern and western areas became the 'New Reich', annexed to the 'Third Reich', Hitler's remodelled German state. Central and southern areas were formed into a separate 'General Gouvernement'. Its capital was Krakow, the Polish capital Warsaw having been earmarked for total destruction.

The entire population was obliged to register with the Nazi authorities. First they were racially classified: as Germans, those with German ancestry, non-Germans free of Jewish ancestry, or Jews. Then they were segregated. Those considered suitable for Germanisation were forcibly moved to the 'New Reich' to give them 'German identity'. Many were conscripted into the German army. The Polish language was banned in public and the Catholic Church was persecuted. People deemed 'unsuitable' for Germanisation were herded into the 'General Gouvernement'. Its German Governor Hans Frank wrote: 'All the representatives of the Polish intelligentsia must be killed. It sounds cruel, but it is the right of life. The General Gouvernement is the Polish reservoir, the great Polish Work Camp'.

Special execution squads lost no time in showing this was no idle threat. As well as crushing resistance or opposition, they set about slaughtering entire categories of the population. Between May and August 1940 the 'Extraordinary Pacification Programme' resulted in 10,000 professors, teachers, civil servants and priests being sent to concentration camps, and the mass execution of 3,500 political and municipal leaders in the Palmiry Forest near Warsaw. The 'Euthanasia Campaign' in the same year led to the killing of all mentally and physically disabled people in the country's hospitals. During Nazi occupation Poland lost more than half its lawyers, half its doctors and its engineers, and forty per cent of its university professors. Middle class families had their suburban properties confiscated to provide homes for incoming German officials. All non-Germans were subject to Martial Law which punished any type of offence with death or internment in a concentration camp. Public places were subject to strict racial segregation, with public transport, seating and the better shops and hotels marked 'Germans only'. Non-Germans were confined to their own districts, where they were prohibited from owning a wireless set and were not allowed to congregate in groups of more than three persons, except in church - but all but a handful of churches were closed. Nearly one in five priests was killed. Education above primary level was banned, together with all cultural and artistic activity. Food rationing was introduced which allowed 2,613 calories per day for someone classed as a German, but only 669 for a Pole. The Poles had been classed as fit only for extinction; it was genocide, but on a slow time scale.

Another primary goal of the Nazi war machine was the total obliteration of European Jewry. Prior to the War Poland was a heartland of Jewish culture. A legacy of the relatively tolerant multi-ethnic Polish Commonwealth, it had the largest concentration of Jews anywhere in the world. From the outset, Nazi occupation was marked by intermittent massacres and the passing of laws which stripped Jews of all human and economic rights. During 1940 Jewish families from nearly 2,000 towns and cities were forced to move into labour camps or enclosed ghettos in a few cities. The Warsaw Ghetto crammed half a million people, including deportees from Germany and Austria, into an area that had previously housed 35,000. Although abandoned to a world of starvation, disease and summary executions, the inhabitants of the Ghetto established secret schools, hospitals and other self-help and cultural organisations.

However the Germans were unhappy with the amount of time it was taking to work and starve people to death, and looked for more efficient methods than simply shooting people. The first experiments in mass extermination by gassing took place in 1941. In addition to the labour camps, usually attached to military sites, camps dedicated solely to the task of killing people were built in the General Gouvernement. Auschwitz, Belzec, Chelmno, Majdanek, Sobibor and Treblinka were

Suitcases belonging to people transported to Auschwitz concentration camp near Krakow.

Janina Struk.

"The children had lost their parents, and the parents had lost their children, and husbands had lost their wives and wives had lost their husbands. It was... the cry, I can still hear the crying in my ears; I think that was the worst, the worst wailing I ever heard."

"When we arrived in Auschwitz we all had to get out, and then you had the doctor there who selected us, who looked at people, and when he saw you might be useful for work you went to one side, and if you were old or ill looking you went to the other side. And luckily I went with the young and so-called healthy women. I made myself big and tall and strong, you soon realised it was probably wise to do so. So, from what I remember, nobody was over thirty; I never met anybody over thirty after that."

'factories of death' where Jews were brought from all over Europe, together with hundreds of thousands of Poles, Russians, gypsies and other peoples. In 1943 the remaining Jews in the Warsaw Ghetto led the first mass revolt against Hitler, but after an unequal battle lasting twenty-seven days the few survivors were taken to Treblinka. Out of 3.35 million Polish Jews, only 340,000 were alive by the end of the War, most of them refugees in the Soviet Union.

Despite foreign occupation Poles were able to form an underground state operating its own legal system and courts. Over a million children were educated in secret schools, and the universities of Warsaw, Krakow, Lwow and Wilno all operated underground. The official resistance organisation, the Home Army, was commanded by the exiled government in London. By 1944, with 400,000 members, it was the largest resistance unit in Europe.

The turning point of the War came with the defeat of the German army at Stalingrad in December 1942, and in 1943 it was the turn of the Red Army to advance through Polish territory. Rising up against the disintegrating Germans the Home Army played an important role in liberating many Polish cities such as Wilno and Lwow. However their military successes were not matched by political ones. Their aim was to welcome the Soviets into a free Polish state whose government would then return from London. The Soviet leaders simply denounced the Polish government-in-exile, recognised as the legitimate authority on Polish matters by everyone else, and confined their dealings to people appointed by themselves. As the Red Army advanced, the Polish resistance emerged to fight alongside them, only to end up under arrest by the Soviets. The Poles assumed that Stalin would respect pre-war frontiers. He had no intention of doing so, and with Poland unrepresented at the Tehran conference held to decide the fate of post-war Europe, the Americans and the British had colluded with Russia in a secret decision to move Poland westwards at the end of the War.

The greatest act of resistance carried out by the Home Army was the Warsaw Rising against the Nazis on 1st August, 1944, when the Soviet army was poised to enter the city. The Home Army leader, Bor-Komorowski, believed that Polish-led liberation of Warsaw would not only strike a blow against the Germans, but also legitimise the government-in-exile's claim to govern Poland and 'mobilise the entire population spiritually for the struggle against Russia'. The Home Army expected that Soviet troops would come to their aid: but for two months, the Red Army watched and waited on the edge of the city. Unaided, the Poles fought on in what has been described as the most heroic, and by far the bloodiest, urban insurrection that Europe has ever seen. 150,000 poorly-armed men and women faced the full might of the Nazis. The Germans drove rows of civilians in front of their advancing troops and roped women and children to the sides of tanks to deter attacks, while their artillery and air bombardment reduced the city to rubble. The Warsaw Rising ended in defeat and the deaths of 245,000 inhabitants. Hitler ordered that the city should be 'razed without trace,' and those buildings which remained were dynamited. 700,000 survivors were transported to forced labour and concentration camps. When the Soviet Army finally entered the gutted city in January 1945 over 90 per cent of its buildings were destroyed and the city was empty.

Unquestionably, the decision to launch the Rising was taken for honourable motives, but historians consider it a tragic mistake. The exiled government was irreparably damaged, politically, militarily and psychologically. The underground in Poland disintegrated rapidly. Following in the footsteps of the victorious Red Army came a new government, the Soviet-backed Polish Committee of National Liberation, formed in Moscow and led by an unknown communist of whom most Poles had never heard. As the front line moved westwards, this government granted control of security to the NKVD - the secret police, forerunners of the KGB. They imposed a régime familiar to those who had experienced the Soviet invasion of 1939. All local officials were replaced. Members of the Home Army were imprisoned in former concentration camps, and their leaders put on trial as 'saboteurs and subversionist bandits'. Livestock and foodstores were ruthlessly requisitioned. Anyone who dissented was locked up or simply added to the toll of war dead. By the time peace was declared in May 1945 the whole of the country lay under Soviet rule, and the Soviet army was to remain on Polish soil for over forty years.

The occupying Nazi régime ruled Poland by terror and executions such as this were common. Although certain groups were targeted, the selection of many of the victims was arbitrary.

IWM.

"You go to buy something and you don't know if you come back home or not. They would close the one street and there is a lorry and people are taken. But people must go out, must work. But if you go into town you don't know if you come back."

"So we were afraid already of the Germans, but nothing we could do. We heard on the radio all the speeches that Hitler had given, threatening speeches. It didn't mention specifically Jews, but he was hating the Poles, the Polish nation. He compared them to animals."

"There was, on the walls in the town, everywhere, new regulations. For example if you saw a German walking on the pavement a hundred yards away you should get off the pavement; and if you wore a hat, as you see the Germans you take the hat off. And they snatched people off the streets, and sent them away, we didn't know where."

Polish partisans near Wilno in occupied Poland. At its height the Home Army numbered 400,000. Organised in small groups they carried out assassinations, acts of sabotage, and set up a hugely successful intelligence service for the Allies.

IWM.

"The worst part was... they didn't know you were in the underground Army, you kept it away from your family. My mother probably had a kind of a feeling, she asked me once or twice if I'm involved. You told very few people, you didn't tell your wife."

Member of the German army chatting with fellow Poles after his surrender to the Allies. Poles classed as having German ancestry were often forced to enlist, but many later changed sides. By the end of the war 35,000 men in the Polish Second Corps had previously served in the German army.

Sikorski Museum.

"Germans were needing men for their army so they were looking in family trees, and if they find German blood they made you sign as German third class. My father didn't want to be a German, but four SS men came to see him. They said they found some German blood in our family tree and they give him forty-eight hours to sign. He wouldn't, but asked me what to do. I said 'Well, what can you do, you have to sign it'. I and my brother were over sixteen and I said, 'They can take us, but you, mother and two sisters will be safe, we'll go to front. You can take a horse to water but they can't make it drink. They can take me to battle but I don't have to fight'. In my case it was so, but in my brother's case it was different, he fell. Week before his seventeenth birthday."

The identity photograph of Genowesa Sobucka, now living in Sheffield, who was taken to Germany as a slave labourer. By 1944 there would be 5.7 million foreign workers in Germany, 87% of them from areas east of the country.

BHRU.

"I went because you had to, because otherwise the Germans would burn the house, would take father, take everybody... I had to go, no choice. 1942, I were sixteen. They bring us to a factory in Opladen... making parachutes... I was using a lot of bleach and I had red hands, swollen all the time. People were drinking the methylated spirits. It was poison, but people drank it and died through that. I was very poorly but I didn't bother for my life in Germany, I wouldn't have minded if I were dead. When you're like this, you're not bothered."

All citizens were obliged to register with the Nazi authorities. First they were racially classified and then they were segregated. Jews were forced to live in enclosed ghettos created in towns, such as this one in Warsaw.

Sikorski Museum.

"I had quite a lot of friends who were Christians, being in a school where I was the only Jewish child. They were very, very kind to me. Of course the anti-Semitism started and they used to put pickets in front of the Jewish shops. They used to wait near the trains where the Jewish boys were coming, and they used to beat them up. I was very, very lucky in a way, because my father was rather a tough man and nobody would dare touch me."

"We went into hiding, like Anne Frank. Our area in the ghetto was getting emptied out, and we had a neighbour that was in the Jewish police force, he hid his family. He had built a secret wall into one room, and he put his wardrobes flush against the wall... It didn't have no windows, it only had a door, and he locked it... Close to sixteen or eighteen people, and during the day we laid like mice... You lived like on a volcano, you think you are going to blow up any minute because your stomach is so full of nerves, from fear, and they're emptying out the building, and the Gestapo standing in the street with dogs. The trams are ready for our building, and we hear all this going on, the shouting and the yelling... And it's getting quiet, we can hear the trams chuk-chuk-chuk away. And a neighbour of ours came out of hiding, she wanted to cook and when she made a fire it smoked. So of course, they know there's people still in the buildings. They come rushing back, and we were discovered."

The Warsaw Ghetto, where by February 1942 50,000 Polish Jews had starved to death. In April 1943 liquidation of the Ghetto was delayed by a month by an armed revolt. 7,000 Jews died in the fighting, and 30,000 were deported to Treblinka.

Sikorski Museum.

"One day two SS men came. And I had my rucksack always ready there, and my mother was lying there and I just stood in the door. I was afraid even to go to say to her, to say goodbye. I just stood in the doorway and I said, 'Mama, Gottchen be with us,' and so I left. I don't know what happened to her at all. They took me to the wagons there, and the wagons were full of people."

"When we got to Auschwitz, they started separating women from men. It was just terrible. Husbands from wives, mothers from sons, it was just a nightmare. I was sick, and diarrhoea suddenly. We started going through the gate, the SS men on both sides. People could see what state I was in, and they started to put sugar in my mouth to revive me. They were just holding me up, and it was left and right, left and right. They told me to go to the right, the SS men... It was dark, and they are starting to march us. And can you imagine the screams? The mother was going to the left, the daughter was going to the right; the babies going to the left, the mothers going to the right... Oy oy! I cannot explain to you the cries and the screams, and tearing their hair off. Can you imagine?"

Children behind the electric fence at Auschwitz concentration camp in Poland. One of the Nazis' largest death camps, its vast gas chambers and crematoria could slaughter up to 15,000 people per day. Auschwitz alone accounted for nearly three million dead.

Weiner Library.

"I saw horrible things in Auschwitz... there was a very big hole, twenty metres long, three, four, metres wide and four metres deep, and cement all round. Lorry comes, backs into this and children, full of children, maybe ten, twelve years old. Alive, without gas, they shovel them on fire. Even now, many time when I'm going to sleep, I don't know why, this memory come to my eyes, this cruelty. Only seconds, these children screaming, when they gone on fire... when I'm talking to you I see this black smoke, coming from fire, then quiet, nothing more."

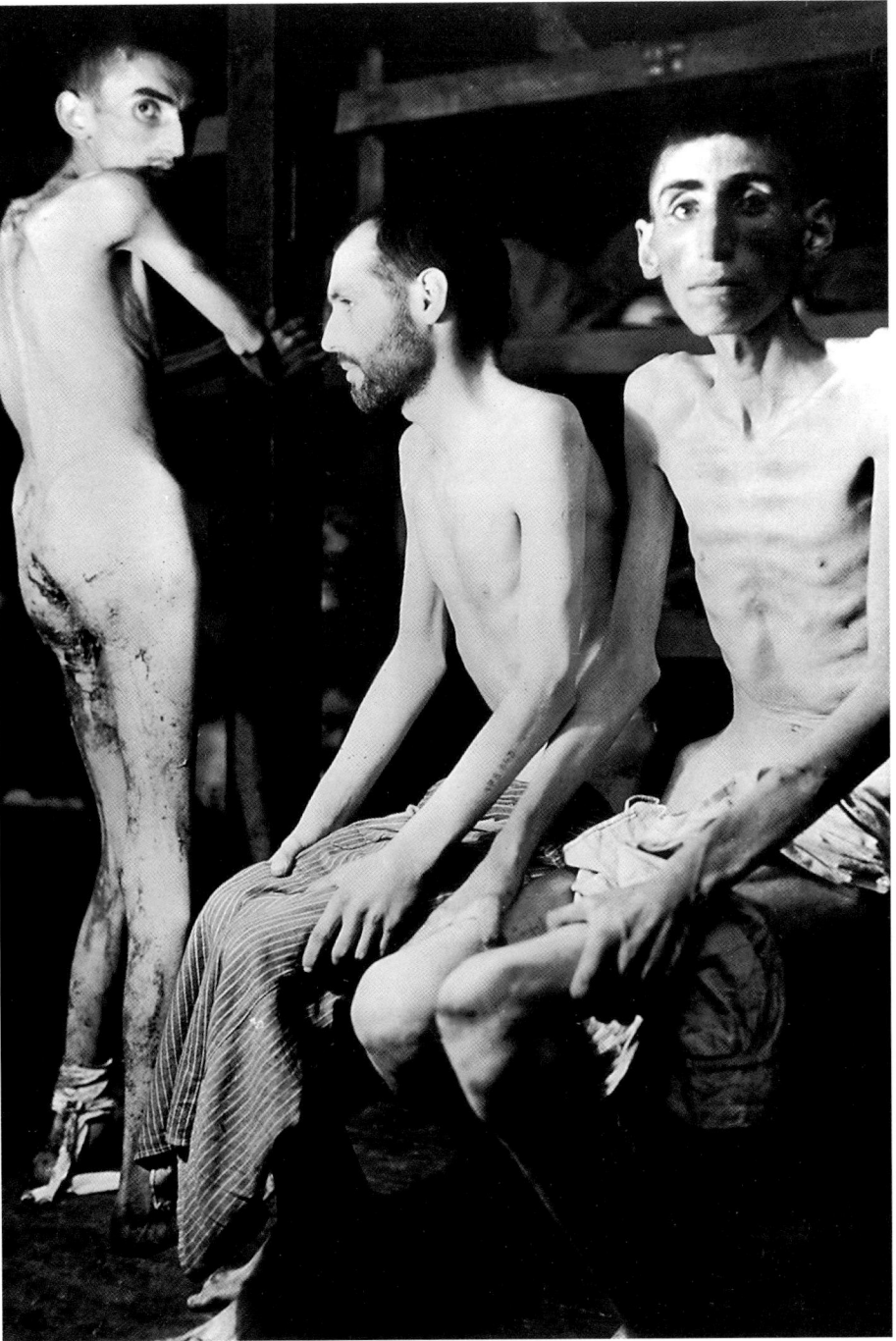

Buchenwald, one of the original concentration camps which were built as places of internment or punishment. As the Nazi terror accelerated in 1941, many of the camps in this vast network became centres for systematic genocide.

IWM.

"Auschwitz was hell, but Belsen was living hell, because there you just wasted away, you... There we got even less to eat, there was absolute starvation, and people were dying in their hundreds overnight. The piles of dead bodies lying all over the place. I saw such things I couldn't believe."

"When it was getting lighter I could see there are like blocks, and a girl comes out, she has no shoes, she has no hair, her dress is far above the knee. I thought maybe some children, some girls got mad and they're keeping them together in a mad house, not thinking that in a couple of hours time I would look exactly the same. All the time sorting, sorting, sorting. Who knew what they were doing? They were sorting to put in the gas chambers, but who knew it? I still was very ignorant, I still did not know what was waiting. And eventually they put us in another place where they started shaving us everywhere, washing us in showers, and giving us dresses, just dresses, nothing else. And I knew why the dresses were getting shorter and shorter, because when you went to the toilet it didn't have no paper so we were tearing the dresses off, to wipe ourselves."

Polish, Russian and Dutch prisoners peer from their bunks at Buchenwald concentration camp in Germany. Thousands of Polish politicians, teachers and civil servants were taken here in 1939. Nine hundred prisoners died each day during the winter which followed.

IWM.

"In Auschwitz... this Kapo once told us, for killing one person he received a double portion of bread and margarine... he is speaking Polish, he was born in Poland. And he said, 'Do you know who I am? I am past law, I am past God, I can do with you what I want to'."

As the end of the War approached the Nazis began to force many of their surviving prisoners on 'death marches' from Poland to Germany. Many froze or starved to death or were shot. Here, at Gardelegen, over 300 were killed after being herded into a barn which was set alight.

Sikorski Museum.

"And they built scaffolding to be hanged. And this incident, I remember clearly now...They picked a day when we didn't go to work, I don't know what day it was. The whole camp had to come out, and they built it so high, the scaffolding, that everybody should see, and the Germans said, 'Let that be a lesson to anyone who thinks to escape'. And they were hung one by one. Some of them insulted the Germans, some of them sang the National Anthem for Poland. And they were hanging there for a few nights, a few days."

Members of the Home Army prepare for the Warsaw Rising which began on 1st August 1944. For sixty-three days the 'Home Army' of 30,000 poorly-armed men and women faced the full might of the Nazi war machine.

Sikorski Museum.

"Before the actual uprising started we were all on alert. When it started... I came home to gather a few things... basic food for a day or two. We had grenades, it was a very little army, but rebels hoped to be able to get things from Germans when the fighting started."

Captured members of the Home Army are marched off to prisoner-of-war camps. Including civilian casualties, the Warsaw Rising cost 200,000 Polish lives.

Sikorski Museum.

"I remember from the Warsaw uprising. We were without water, we had to dig wells in the road. We had German prisoners there and we took them to do the digging... Of course we took German prisoners during the uprising. Apart from the SS men they were well treated. But the SS, why not? Often they were just shot and that was it because a lot of us suffered badly and that was the pay back."

Dr Bartoszewski and Countess Tarnowska of the Polish Red Cross approach German lines across the shattered square of the University of Warsaw. Acting on behalf of the commander of the Home Army, General Bor-Komorowski, they carry the white flag of surrender.

IWM.

"Russians were on other side of the Vistula River, and wouldn't give us help. We thought we might win at first but after four or five weeks we knew we were going to lose it... Every day was fighting, then the Germans attacked with tanks, and after that, no chance. For the last two weeks we had no water, no food."

Inmates at Dachau concentration camp near Munich cheer US Army troops who liberated them on 30th April 1945.

IWM.

"We had to walk. Well I don't know how many miles it was from Flossenberg to Dachau. It was long, say thirty kilometres a day and it was about six days we were walking... It must have been bad because at the end of it, from the six thousand, four thousand were left. One of my friends died during the march. There was just froth coming from his mouth. He lost consciousness and couldn't walk. We dragged him so far, but had to leave him simply because we didn't have the strength. We used to chew grass, slugs, anything. When you're hungry it's surprising what you can eat. You had to drink where you could find any water. They wouldn't allow anybody to give you any water. Mind you, the majority of people used to be spitting at us, shouting and all, when we passed villages. Only at one place, a middle-aged German lady with her daughter, came out with a bucket of clean water. But the guard kicked it away, because that was the purpose of the march, to kill as many of us as possible."

During the chaos at the end of the war people hunt for missing relatives and friends by way of notices displayed on street corners.

Sikorski Museum.

"My husband was taken to Germany as a prisoner-of-war and we were corresponding. And 1945, the War ended, so I thought my husband will come home now. And I was waiting every day, because there were loads of trains coming with soldiers from all over the world, and nothing. He chose to go to Italy because Poland is under occupation, and I didn't hear from him for a year, I didn't know a thing. In May 1946 I got a letter giving me an address in Warsaw. A soldier in the Polish army is collecting officers' wives and smuggling them to Germany. Three months after I started in Poland I got to Italy."

Churchill, Roosevelt and Stalin, leaders of the 'Big Three' Allied powers, at the Yalta conference in 1945. Poland was not represented at these talks, and a new era of Soviet occupation of the country was agreed.

IWM.

SETTLING IN BRITAIN

Six million Polish citizens died during the War. Their army had been the first to resist Hitler, Britain had declared war in defence of Polish independence, and Polish forces had fought to defend Britain. Despite all this, as the Allies celebrated their victory at the end of the Second World War, Poland was dealt a series of shattering blows. The Soviet Army arrived in Warsaw with a ready-made government in tow. Democratic elections were promised by Stalin 'within months' of the end of the War. They were eventually held in 1947, and after widespread intimidation and arrests of opposition party members and candidates, an overwhelming victory was announced for the unpopular Soviet-backed régime.

The War had brought deep and lasting changes to the country ruled over by this new régime. Plans for post-war Europe had been drawn up by the 'Big Three' Allied powers at the conferences of Tehran (1943) and Yalta (1945). The Americans and British had bowed to Stalin's demands, and with the defeat of the Germans, Poland was moved bodily 150 miles to the west. Although the 'Recovered Lands' in the west of this new Poland had been taken from Germany, half of the Poles' pre-war territory had been incorporated into the Soviet Union, including the cities of Wilno and Lwow. Polish communities in these eastern areas were expelled from the Soviet Union to repopulate towns in Poland and in the Recovered Lands from which the German inhabitants had been removed. This process, coupled with the incorporation of Ukraine and Byelorussia into the Soviet Union and the virtual extinction of Polish Jewry, meant that Polish-speaking Roman Catholics were now in an overwhelming majority. For the first time in its history, the Polish state comprised a nation of ethnic Poles sharing a common religion, albeit one ruled over by a government controlled by its traditional enemies in Moscow.

At the end of the War the rest of Europe was awash with people displaced from their homes. Over a million were Poles, half of them in British zones of occupation. They included members of the Polish armed forces, refugees who had fled the Nazi or Soviet armies, people forced into slave labour or into the German army, survivors of concentration camps and the Warsaw Rising, and other prisoners-of-war. Some had also managed to escape from Soviet zones of occupation, including Poland itself. Polish military units acted as magnets, particularly the bases of 'Anders' Army' who had ended the War in northern Italy. There were also civilians who had escaped Stalin's labour camps scattered in camps throughout the British Empire. Like the members of 'Anders' Army,' these civilians' former homes in eastern Poland were now part of the Soviet Union, and they went on to form the majority of the community who finally settled in Britain.

All Poles abroad feared - with justification - that they would be viewed as enemies of the Communist régime should they return to Poland. Most already had first-hand experience of Stalin's prisons and labour camps. Post-war trials in Moscow of Polish military and political leaders for 'offences against the law of the Russian Republic' were widely publicised in the West, while other Polish officials simply disappeared. Deciding where to go was a long and painful process, particularly for those whose families were still in Poland. Pressure built up in emigre circles; to go back could be seen as a vote for the new régime in Poland and a betrayal of the nationalist cause. Eventually 105,000 Polish soldiers did return to Poland. The rest settled in the West, mainly in the USA and Canada. 140,000 made Britain their home in spite of the efforts of the British government to persuade them to go back to Poland. The new Labour administration, and particularly the Foreign Secretary Ernest Bevin, put less emphasis on Churchill's Anglo-American alliance, wanting instead to become a mediating force between East and West. They withdrew recognition from the Polish government-in-exile in London, and supported the Warsaw Communist government in persuading the Polish army to return. In a message to all members of the Polish forces under British command, Bevin wrote in March 1946 of their 'patriotic duty' to return to their 'liberated' home country. The attitude of the expatriate Poles differed considerably, remaining loyal to their

Poles in German prisoner-of-war camps at the end of the war. Many of those released sought out Polish units stationed in Germany, or travelled south to make contact with those who had fought in Italy.

Sikorski Museum.

"Settlement in Britain was made all the more difficult by our feeling of betrayal. The Yalta, Tehran and Potsdam treaties seemed, especially to those who'd served in the British services, as a betrayal. We felt extreme bitterness towards our allies, who recognised the puppet Polish government which was killing people who'd fought for the freedom of our country. The withdrawal of recognition of the legitimate Polish government-in-exile was a bitter blow. We were completely lost and this didn't help us to settle. We didn't trust our allies any more and no longer felt safe."

"We knew that Poland was sold to the Russians. Churchill and Roosevelt, they sold us down the drain. We knew we couldn't go back. It was painful, very painful."

"My mother felt that Poland was completely sold down the river at Yalta, she has an unshakeably clear view that the Allies just sold out, and Poland was the price that had to be paid."

government-in-exile. Feelings of despair, humiliation and anger were further compounded when, in an effort by the British government to appease Stalin, the Polish army was deliberately excluded from the London Victory Parade held on the 6th June 1946. Only twenty-five Poles - members of the Polish Air Force - were invited to take part, and these withdrew from the parade in solidarity with their countrymen.

Ultimately the British conceded that wholesale repatriation was unfeasible and began to ship Poles to Britain. Military units from Italy arrived in 1946, followed by troops from Germany and the Middle East in 1947, to be joined by their dependents and other civilians. They came to a country badly in need of reconstruction with an acute labour shortage. The British government recognised that far from being an awkward problem, the Poles could represent a vital labour force. A further 14,000 Poles were actively recruited from Displaced Persons camps on the continent under the European Voluntary Workers scheme, along with other foreign nationals such as Ukrainians. Jews of any nationality were excluded, the government citing 'a real risk of a wave of anti-Semitic feeling in this country'. Not for the first (or last) time the anticipation of anti-Semitism was used to justify anti-Semitic policies, and less than 2,000 survivors of European Jewry, including Poles, were able to enter Britain after the War.

Polish ex-servicemen already in Britain found attitudes towards them changed with the ending of the War. Once British forces were demobilised, the sight of Poles still in uniform provoked a widespread response of: 'Why don't you go home?'. They were no longer seen as valiant allies, and in many quarters (including the popular press) they were labelled 'black marketeers,' 'womanisers' and 'anti-Soviet war-mongers'. Despite the shortage of manpower they were also seen as a threat to British jobs, and like many other European immigrants they suffered obstruction from trades unions hostile to their recruitment.

Demobilisation of the Polish troops was seen as a priority, and the Polish Resettlement Corps was created as a transitional stage to civilian life in Britain, providing accommodation, English tuition, and training. After two years of ordered camp life Poles had to move into the civilian world. They were initially restricted to working in agriculture, coal-mining, textiles, hotels, construction, and the steel industry. Most found themselves in jobs completely alien to them. Many of those from rural backgrounds found themselves working in urban environments. Those who had arrived with professional experience (apart from doctors and pharmacists whose qualifications were recognised) had to take on manual jobs. These problems were added to those of a strange language and culture. Leaflets entitled 'To help you settle in England' were produced by the Ministry of Labour, and included advice on queuing, using the word 'sorry,' and dissuading men from kissing a woman's hand. Most Poles relied on each other's support to see them through the first difficult years of their new lives in exile.

Several factors made the Poles a unique group amongst post-war immigrants to Britain. For the most part, they arrived in well-organised groups including schools and hospitals as well as military units. They had their own political and military leadership and a significant cultural and literary élite. Although economic factors played a role in their decision to settle in Britain, the community perceived themselves as political exiles. During the early days many viewed life in Britain as a temporary state of affairs. The development of the Cold War was seen as a preface to inevitable armed conflict between the West and Communism. This would renew the Western allies' recognition of the Polish government-in-exile, which would ultimately return home leading a liberation army.

This early hope of a short exile followed by triumphant return to the homeland was unfulfilled, and Poles were to live in Britain longer than they could ever have imagined. Despite this the aims of the community remained remarkably consistent. While the Communist regime in Poland was intent on destroying Polish society, these exiles would maintain and develop Polish culture and foster independent political thought. They would support struggles by the Church and non-Communist intellectuals within Poland itself, but in helping to preserve and carry forward the nation's history and its collective memory, they intended to become the true voice of an independent Poland.

These women are newly-released slave labourers who had been working in Germany. A mixture of Poles, Ukrainians, Russians, Byelorussians and others, they had to undergo a screening process to decide their fate. Many hoped to remain in the West to avoid Soviet reprisals, but it had been agreed by the Allies that former citizens of the Soviet Union would be returned to their homelands. There they would probably be imprisoned or executed, accused of 'collaboration' with the Germans.

Sikorski Museum.

"Because I was a barrister, after the War I was engaged by the British government. My main task was to select [who would be granted passage to Britain and who would be sent back to places controlled by Stalin]. There were many Ukrainians, from Russian Ukraine, who were still in Germany. They spoke a bit of Polish, and learned it is better to say 'I am from Lwow'. But [to find out if they were from Lwow] I would ask 'In Lwow, what colour were the trams?', and I selected. The Ukrainians that were sent back to Ukraine were mostly shot. Perhaps we were a bit dirty but it wasn't our responsibility, you have to do it. Difficult decision."

Refugees housed in a Displaced Persons camp, many of which were set up to deal with the huge numbers of foreigners whom the Allies found in Germany at the end of the War.

Sikorski Museum.

"We stayed a few months in Italy waiting for transport to England. There were thousands of people there, families, a lot came from the east, through Russia... And they congregated there, everybody was waiting. I went to a special camp for families and waited there. My husband was sent to Napoli because there was officers' transport going to Glasgow and they agreed to take him... We went by train to Calais where we boarded a ferry to Dover. Then they took us to a camp in Horsham."

"A lot of people who did go back to Poland, you never heard about them, since they were shot or sent off to Siberia. So a lot of people were in fear of going back home. Also there was a lot of guilt, families that had been left behind in much poorer circumstances. My mum's area that she came from, they owned quite a lot of land. Well, that was all collectivised, so it no longer belonged to her family, her mother was left in terribly reduced circumstances. So economically it wasn't such a good idea. Politically it would have been suicide for a lot of them."

"We stayed on as part of the Rhine Army for two-and-a-half years, helping the Displaced Persons. We organised schools for the youngsters and prepared them for a new life in a new country. And they emigrated all over the world, Canada, America, Australia, New Zealand, Italy, and many went back to Poland as well. I had the papers ready to go to America, but thinking of my wife and daughter in Poland, I thought it's much further to America than Britain, so I thought it was better to come here."

A train leaves northern Italy carrying members of the Second Corps who had opted to return to Poland.

IWM.

"I wanted to go back, but friends said, 'For goodness sake, don't go back because you'll be arrested there'. If you go there and they know you escaped from the Russians they will take you to jail and they will send you to Russia. I didn't go back at all. I have never been back."

"My friend went back and he told me, 'I write to you a letter, no matter what I put to you in the letter, if I write by ink come back, if I write by pencil, don't'. He didn't write by ink or pencil, he was locked up straight away, so I changed my mind and didn't go."

"A good friend of mine, with whom I had many conversations before he decided to go back, was of this opinion, that we ought to go and then somehow fight from within. He stayed in the forces about a year, and then they accused him of working against the state and he was executed... Many, many were sent to concentration camps and no one has heard of them ever since."

Transport of orphans from camps in India organised by members of the Polish Red Cross.

BHRU.

"Places were offered for War orphans by other countries apart from Britain, but the government-in-exile discouraged this, 'The youth would be lost to the nation'. So in the end they came here, and the aim was to return to Poland eventually."

Members of the Polish Armed Forces arriving in Britain at the end of the War.

Sikorski Museum.

"Bevin, the Minister of the British Foreign Office, he wrote a letter to each Polish soldier, advising them to go back to Poland, although it was under occupation... Everybody read this letter and laughed at it. Very funny... Few, less than ten percent, went to Poland. Those who were left then received a letter, that if any of you, for political or any other reason, refuse to go to Poland, we offer hospitality in Great Britain."

"At the end of the War, a friend said there were jobs in Manchester. So I got on a train and was told to get off at the first big city. But not understanding English, I got off the train in Sheffield. It was a mistake but I remembered in Poland, forks had 'Sheffield' on them, so I decided to stay. I never thought I'd end up in the place where cutlery comes from."

"I had always been told that Britain was a very well-off country where everybody has a grammar school education, and that it is a country where everybody should want to go and stay. Well, when we came here we found it all entirely different. Of course it was just after the War, and there were so many men being demobbed, but you could see the poverty when you got here."

Refugee children, many of them orphans, came to Britain as pupils of schools which arrived in their entirety from all over the British Empire. The language of tuition was Polish, and many children spoke additional languages, such as Russian or Swahili, depending on where they had come from.

Sikorski Museum.

"I was very upset when I arrived... I didn't know people my age and I cried and cried. I said to my Mum, 'I'm going to run away'. But Mum was explaining that it's one of those things, you got to settle, you got to work at it, 'Eventually you'll learn English and be happy'."

"They gave me food I never had in my life, beans on toast... it's not good."

"My mother, even now after forty years, she doesn't speak that much English. She depended on us. I was five and I couldn't speak English until I went to school. I can remember very early on taking over letter writing, administration, I'd do everything."

The Polish Resettlement Corps was set up in 1946 to ease the move into British civilian life for members of the armed forces, their dependants, and the large numbers of civilian refugees who had joined them.

Janina Struk.

"I signed for two years with the Polish Resettlement Corps and they asked me what station I wanted to go to, so I said Scampton would do for me. If I'd had a bad record they would have sent me to the Isle of Man or somewhere out of the way. My friend went to the Isle of Man because he had a bad record. He used to make Polish sausages and sell them in the mess room, which the English wouldn't allow. Black pudding, all sorts, and they were nice."

POLISH RESETTLEMENT CORPS
(ROYAL AIR FORCE)

POLSKI KORPUS PRZYSPOSOBIENIA
I ROZMIESZCZENIA
(ROYAL AIR FORCE)

CONDITIONS OF SERVICE
(KEY)

WARUNKI SŁUŻBY
(TEKST POLSKI; ANGIELSKI)

RESTRICTED

The information given in this document is not to be communicated, either directly or indirectly, to the Press or to any person not authorised to receive it.

Tylko do użytku służbowego.

Przepisy zawarte w niniejszej instrukcji nie mogą być ujawnione bezpośrednio lub pośrednio prasie ani też żadnej nie uprawnionej do tego osobie.

THE AIR MINISTRY.
OCTOBER 1946.
PAŹDZIERNIK 1946.

Many of those in the Polish Resettlement Corps were housed in former military camps spread all over the country. They often lived in barrel-like Nissan huts, as seen here.

BHRU.

"In 1946 my son was born in the camp. We were living in a Nissan hut and it was lovely. Oh, I was so happy. We had an Officers' Mess, so we went for lunch, for breakfast and for supper. And it was such a social life, because it was all together. And suddenly after two years they said, 'Finish, no more army, now you have to disappear into the English community and do whatever you like'. And it was very hard. Everything was on the ration you see, and now we are civilians, what to do? We didn't know the language."

The vast majority of Poles knew no English at the end of the War, and one of the main tasks of the Polish Resettlement Corps was the teaching of the language.

Sikorski Museum.

"The English language is quite difficult to learn, the grammar is different. I probably learned quicker because I knew German. I had a very good teacher as well. This parson was teaching us English and he was beautifully spoken, he was Cambridge educated, the way he spoke really fascinated me."

"I joined the travelling library, because I was in a village. Once a week you could choose the books, and I was reading books with a dictionary, and I came to the moment that I didn't need a dictionary. But I couldn't speak it and I didn't understand people because I had no pronunciation, that is what is so difficult for Polish people."

"The problem of communication is this, that the Polish people here, with a few exceptions, didn't see any need in learning the English language in the very beginning. Maybe they didn't have the opportunity, because if you're a miner, or if you work in textiles, in dust and noisy conditions, who do you talk to? To nobody, you talk to yourself. Then when you come home to your Polish wife, or to your Polish husband for that matter, you converse in the language which is the easiest for you. I think it is also true that some Poles lived with the hope that one day, sooner or later, the Polish question would be resolved and everybody would kind of return, so what's the point?"

Dance being held in Edinburgh in the 1940s. There were many more Polish men than women who settled in Britain, which led many to seek partners outside the community.

Sikorski Museum.

"Even though I have British nationality, English people have as a weapon, 'If you don't like it, go back where you come from,' and it hurts. In 1949, with my wife, we went to the pictures and after I said, 'Come on, let's have a drink'. And we went to the Grand Hotel and I was refused a drink because I was a Pole."

"We met at a place called the Palais de Dance in Nottingham. I stood in the entrance of the ballroom looking around for my sister and I couldn't see her. Suddenly this figure in officer's uniform came, clicked his heels, and said, 'Please may I have this dance?' I had a look at him and I thought, 'He's got two stars on his shoulder,' I looked further and saw 'Poland'. I thought, 'Oh my God'. Well at that time there was a lot of propaganda going around about the Poles, that they were very hot blooded, very amorous. And I thought, 'Oh my God, I wish the floor would open up'... Anyway, we got talking in our own way and I arranged to meet him next day for lunch. And from that day to this we've been together."

Poles, and the British women who married them, were registered as 'aliens' at the end of the War, and for many years afterwards had to report to police stations at regular intervals.

Janina Struk.

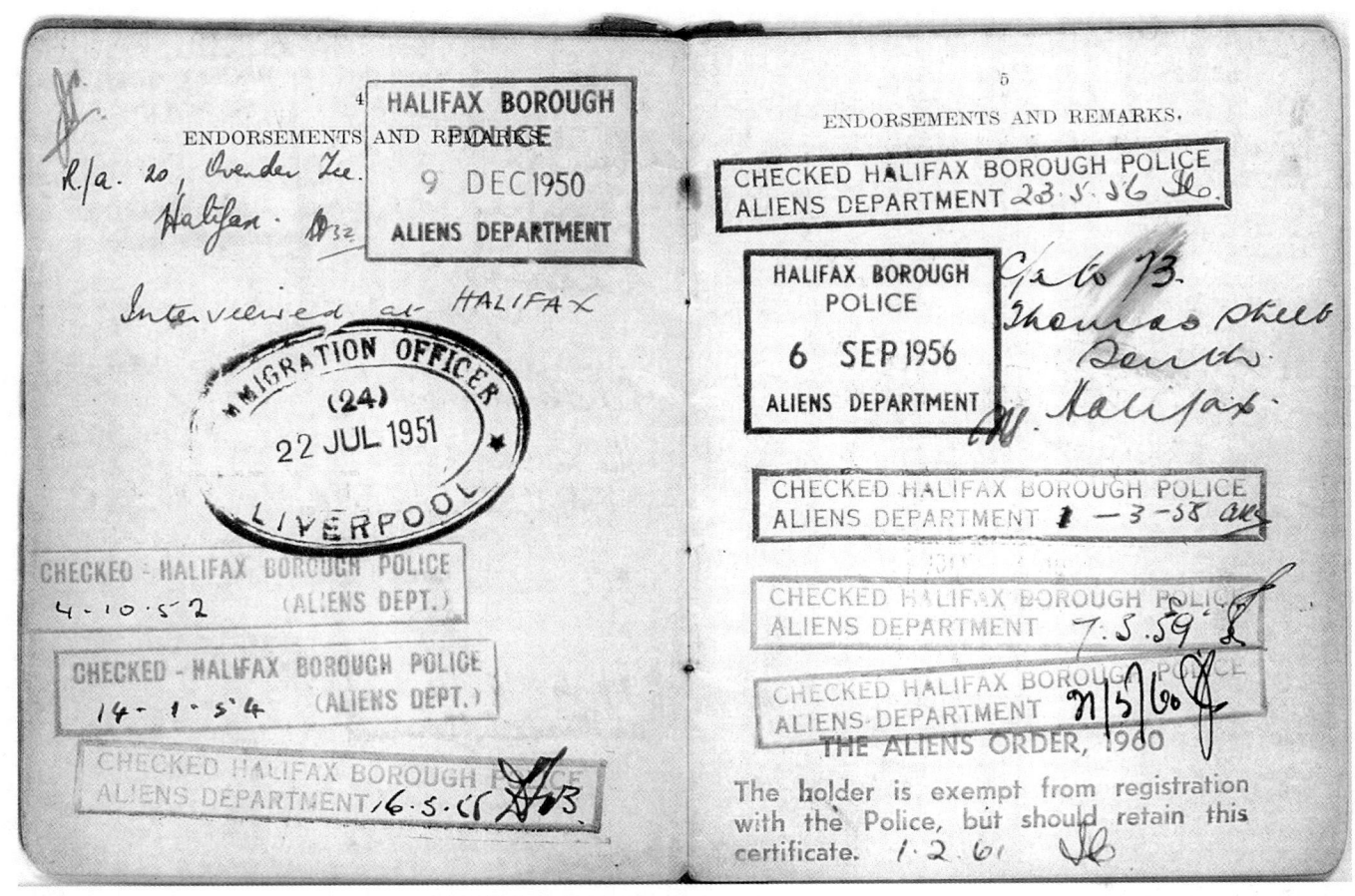

"Those of British origin were not always very pleasant to Poles. We were considered as uninvited guests and I don't wonder because 120,000 arrived in British hostels. But afterwards West Indians arrived, and then those who employed all Poles now employed them. And we were not the lowest class."

"I was refused a job because I was Polish. After training as an engineer I specialised on a milling machine and I went to Laycocks... for a job. They gave me a job straight away but not on a milling machine. I say, 'Why not a milling machine?' 'We will have strike, because you are foreigner.' I say, 'But I know Germans are working on one of milling machines in here.' 'Who tells you that?' I said, 'Never mind, but I know. In that case, stick your job'."

"The matter was raised in Parliament, somebody asked, 'Do you know where all those Poles, and others you absorb, are? Have you got any record of them?'... For two years we were issued a little leaflet by the police and it stated, amongst other things, restrictions. We were not entitled to own our own businesses for the first two years. And if anyone changed address or got married you had to inform the police immediately."

Advertisement for miners in the Polish press in the 1950s. The National Union of Mineworkers was particularly resistant to the employment of foreign workers after the War, but agreement was reached after the government made concessions on working practices.

BHRU.

"I think in the mining community, if they accept you then you're alright. But if they don't accept you then it's a bit of a rough time. On many occasions foreigners had to go to jobs where nobody else wanted to go. Call it the 'market,' a lot of foreigners were on the market... I experienced that... in about four foot, I had knee pads, you had to work on your knees all the time... you couldn't work well because you kept propping up the roof and watching, and many people got killed. There was some jealousy because some jobs were better paid than others. I think I got about £6 a shift, which was pretty good money in the '50s."

"I went down the coal mine, you see they were better paid than anywhere else. And I thought to myself, I'll go there for two or three years. Never been in a coal mine before. Of course, my mother never knew about that... When she did ask me what I was doing I told her that I was going to an engineering firm. Never told her the truth, would have broken her heart. But I just thought, well, it was better money than workers on top."

Many Polish people were recruited to work in the textile industry which was facing a post-war shortage of labour.

Tim Smith.

"In Sheffield... I went to the steel floors. The furnaces were old-fashioned, with coal, so smoky and I were wet through with sweat. Wasn't bad money mind, in 1947, four pounds six and six. But I told myself, 'You big fool, coming here, working for someone, sweating like that'."

"In Bradford there was work available in textiles. A lot of people came here because of that. It wasn't the best kind of work, but it was work. And because on the whole we are good workers, we were offered better and better jobs. Some went up to managers or overlookers or anything like that. I remember a lot of people that I would meet at these Textile Hall dances had bits of fingers cut off and it was like the norm to see that, it was industrial accidents. I remember one chap, his fingers were all different levels. You know when you're small you're sort of fascinated by things like that, aren't you?"

"As long as we work and behave ourselves we never had a problem. Some people say we did but I've never had any problems. I worked with English people, I couldn't speak English, but they were so helpful. If I didn't understand they used to take me by the hand and show me how to do it."

Members of the Polish Resettlement Corps helping to bring in the harvest in Scotland during the 1940s.

Sikorski Museum.

"I am happy here, I made a lot of friends. At times, in British eyes, I am the 'bloody foreigner,' but as soon as they start talking to me they say 'Where are you from?'. I sometimes pull their legs and say 'Scotland'."

"I started work in Leighton Buzzard and Bedford, then I worked in Newbury and from there I moved to Leicester, and from Leicester I moved to Sheffield. At first it was manual, not very nice jobs, because they used to send us to the mines, brickyards, agriculture, and things like that. But eventually, when we learned enough English, we started moving up and taking other positions."

Workers on a hydro-electric scheme on Loch Sloy, near Dunbarton, Scotland, celebrate the completion of building work on a tunnel, 1949.

National Museums of Scotland.

"I thought of going back to Poland, I wanted to be near my family. To repay my mother for all the hard work she had put in, and I knew she wanted me back. I also missed a lot of friends from during the occupation period. I wanted to see what Warsaw looked like, because when I left it was burning. I thought I would be able to help Poland more being over there. And perhaps, looking at it today, that would have been true. But would I have got through? It was very difficult at that time, a lot of people were being arrested for having been in the Polish underground [Home] Army, and being persecuted by the Communists. I never knew what would have happened if I'd gone back and probably that was what stopped me from going. I thought something will eventually crop up... but then things dragged and dragged, and I got to my thirties and was settled and nothing had happened, then it was too late to go back. Many people went and settled, some regretted it and some didn't. I wanted to go back more when my mother was alive. But I didn't achieve anything, that was the worst part. I didn't want to disappoint her because she thought about me so highly, that I'd make something of my life [she thought he'd risen through the ranks in the army]. Actually I didn't achieve anything, I was just a hard-working miner."

A woman born in Britain holds the only two possessions her mother brought here. They are her Polish bible, and a photograph of her holding the bible on the farm in Germany where she worked during the War.

Tim Smith.

DEVELOPMENT OF THE COMMUNITY

By the end of 1949 the vast majority of Poles who were to settle here had already arrived in Britain. A Home Office report estimated numbers at around 162,000 people, the majority being former deportees to the Soviet Union. The Polish Resettlement Act, passed by the British Government in 1947, acknowledged that the Poles were here to stay, and allocated roles for the Ministries of Labour, Health, Education and Pensions in providing for their needs and assisting assimilation. Although the British authorities were keen to see the Poles integrate fully into the British way of life, the community saw their Polishness as something to be preserved. This was felt to be important on a personal level, as well as providing an authentic voice and culture for a Poland ruled by Soviet-backed governments. Maintaining their Polish identity did however become more difficult as people moved out of the camps of the Resettlement Corps, where they had led a secure and regimented life surrounded by fellow Poles, and dispersed into civilian life.

In response to this, a national network of clubs and organisations was set up, their activities co-ordinated by the Federation of Poles in Great Britain. Some, such as the Polish Ex-Combatants' Association (SPK), remain popular with the older generation to this day. Others, such as the Polish Scouts, were aimed at the younger generation. The Saturday School movement was also established as a vital way of instilling in children a sense of pride in their roots through Polish history, language and traditions. By 1960 there were some 150 Polish schools operating attended by 5,000 of the 16,000 children estimated to have been born to Polish parents in Britain. Through these organisations a cohesive identity was maintained, cemented by the bonds of common experience. A wealth of publications was also produced by the community. In the 1940s the *Dziennik Polski* (Polish Daily) had a circulation of 35,000 copies. Today the figure is nearer 7,000.

Where people lived was largely determined by where they could find work and housing. Some communities that had established a base for themselves during the War remained, for example Greater London continued to be the focus of opportunities for the Polish intelligentsia, and still has the largest concentration of Polish-born people in Britain. In other areas lack of work forced people to move. Although communities remain in Glasgow, Edinburgh and other parts of central Scotland, many moved south of the border. Job restrictions enforced during the 1940s confined Poles to 'dirty industries' and had a huge impact on where people came to live. The largest numbers settled in the industrial regions of West Yorkshire, Greater Manchester, the West Midlands and Nottinghamshire, and these remain lively centres of Polish life today. As employment restrictions were lifted during the 1950s, some Poles were able to move into lighter or more rewarding work, although many found this impossible, and remained 'declassed' due to their age, difficulties with language or unrecognised Polish qualifications. The community also moved on as the closely-knit settlements of the early years became more dispersed. The younger generations in particular have tended to move from inner city areas to more middle class residential suburbs, and have now established themselves in a broad range of professions.

The vast majority of those Poles who settled in Britain were members of the Roman Catholic church, which in many ways provided the backbone of the organised Polish community. Those of other Christian denominations, such as the Lutherans, have run their religious affairs separately, but have joined secular Polish organisations. Two percent of Poles who came to Britain were Jewish, but they have tended to identify with Jewish organisations in this country.

The original settlement of Poles consisted mainly of military units, so it is not surprising to find that men outnumbered women by a ratio of three to one. This meant that many men looked for wives outside the Polish community, either British women, or immigrants from

Mr Lominicki who qualified as a barrister in Poland, and after retraining here finished his career as a lecturer at the London School of Economics at the age of 82.

Tim Smith.

"After the war the British government engaged me as an interpreter and representative of Polish interests here. I looked after fifty-five hostels on behalf of the British government. Afterwards, this job shrunk as Poles were settling down. I became a clerical officer for two years and passed then a higher degree in Criminology at the London School of Economics. I became a lecturer at South Bank Polytechnic and I stayed there working until I was eighty-two."

other European countries, especially Italians. Not only were there more Italian women than men in Britain, but a lot of Polish men had spent time in Italy during and after the War, and they shared a common faith in Roman Catholicism. One of the early hostels for European Voluntary Workers in Bradford was run by an Italian-Polish couple who had conducted their courtship and early married life in their only shared language, Latin - that of their church.

By 1956 the régime in Poland had relaxed many of its hardline Stalinist principles. Although this period marked a waning in political involvement amongst the emigre community, the visit to London of the Soviet leader Khrushchev still provoked a demonstration in which 20,000 Poles took part. Some British Poles took advantage of the easing of travel restrictions to visit Poland. Others were staunch in their refusal to go to a country still under foreign domination. Many Poles drew on their savings to bring family members to Britain. Some of these visitors were to stay on a permanent basis, many of them women finding marriage partners here. Husbands and wives who had not seen each other for up to sixteen years were reunited, with mixed success. Fathers were introduced to their children, young men and women whom they had last seen as babies.

The second generation born in Britain were brought up to think of themselves as Poles, but they felt the politics of the *emigracja* of little interest. Many found the stress on tradition stifling, and thought the clubs and institutions had little relevance for them. As a result club membership has declined, although many individuals do maintain the informal links and networks established during their childhood years, considering themselves Polish but not 'belonging' to the Polish community. Many have also married outside the community. There has been some revival of Polish feeling among the young as the profile of Poland has risen. The election of the first Polish Pope, the rise of Solidarity (the driving force behind the independence movement in Poland) and the downfall of Communism all played a part in reviving a sense of pride in Polish roots. It also brought the whole community together and renewed their fundraising and campaigning, resulting in organisations such as the Medical Aid for Poland Fund.

The original settlers believed that one day they would return to an independent Poland. But relatively few of the first generation lived long enough to see the collapse of Communism and the election of Lech Walesa as President in 1989. Fewer still anticipated the speed of events in Poland over this period, and they watched with a mixture of disbelief, anxiety, pride and excitement. After Poland's independence, the government-in-exile which had continued in London was formally dissolved and the Seals of Office, which had left Poland in 1939, were returned to Warsaw.

These changes have also forced the exiles into reassessing their own position and their relationship to their homeland. Does the community in Britain still have a role, and what is its future? The fulfilment of their desire for a free Poland ended their role as political protesters, leaving them in a vacuum. As one community activist was to write: 'There is only one thing worse than losing your homeland: that is, recovering it again after a gap of almost half a century'. These feelings are mitigated by pride that their goals of freedom and an independent nation have been realised, and that the role they played in this has been acknowledged in Poland.

Many of those who did outlive Communist rule have returned on nostalgic and often painful journeys. But for the majority, their former homes now lie in Ukraine, Byelorussia or Lithuania, and the Poland of a new millennium is not the place of idealised childhood memories. Few have gone back to live there permanently. Britain is where their children and grandchildren live, and these younger generations have successfully integrated into British life. Some do maintain loyalties to their Polish culture, and there are many ways in which people can consider themselves Polish, as we hope the quotations in this book may illustrate. However it is the attractions of modern European states - be they Britain or Poland - that are now more relevant to their lives than the traditional concerns of organised community life in this country.

Tea is served in a hostel for Polish women established in a convent in Scotland just after the War

IWM.

"Working overtime... I think it was the thing of the day. The Poles, Ukrainians, everybody was trying to establish themselves at the time and pay off a mortgage. All very, very conscious of having a loan, and they all despised that, and they worked as hard as they could to pay it off as quick as possible. We used to occupy two bedrooms and a kitchen, and the rest of our house was occupied by lodgers. My earliest memories at that time were seeing an awful lot of different people. Each room housed a family."

"I got married and went to live in Oxford. My husband chose Oxford and we lived there for forty-seven years. It was really my country. Oxford is beautiful you know... We were very poor people when we marry after the war. We bought a house and kept lodgers to earn money. Mainly we keep English students because we feel younger and much better with students."

Oak Lane in Manningham, Bradford, 1946. This area was very popular amongst Polish people when they first settled in the city. Like many inner city areas housing was cheap, and close to places of work such as Lister's textile mill which dominated the skyline.

Walter Scott.

"1955, we came to Penistone and it took a few years before we got everything ready. Cooking, ha! That was a problem. I didn't have a cooker, but I still had to do the dinner. I had a fire downstairs and I had a fire upstairs and I had a fire in front room. So I had soup in one room, on the fire I had meat, and on the other fire had potatoes. I were rushing upstairs and downstairs."

"I was born in Bradford. My dad was working here, my mum was in Melton Mowbray. She moved up here when he managed to purchase a house with a £5 deposit on Clarendon Street, just off Lumb Lane. My most vivid memories are of that place, and I don't remember any English people at all. There was a Yugoslavian family, there was a Ukrainian family next door, and I got on really well with their son. There were Polish families up the road, down the road. '56, which is when I remember going to each other's houses, and they used to cook for each other at the beginning. And we used to have loads of lodgers, everybody had lodgers at the time. And then we moved, as did a lot of Polish families, from that area. My dad got a semi-detached house with a garden, which is where he lives now in Shipley. And I had this terrible feeling of everybody stays in their own home, and nobody visits each other."

Procession to mark the festival of Corpus Christi, Edmund Street in Bradford, 1987. As many Polish people found themselves with work that did not meet their qualifications or aspirations, they found an alternative outlet in leadership of the many Polish organisations set up in Britain.

Tim Smith.

"Officers who had been fighting the Germans, they had been doing their best and then suddenly they were reduced to jobs such as lift men in the hotels. They were the 'Silver Brigade,' silver-haired and polishing silver. Because in those days a man over sixty was considered to be old, he couldn't be retrained. How can you explain to a full General in the Polish Army that he can do nothing else but polish?"

"When a British officer was demobbed, very often he had friends in high places and so would get a job as a manager of some sort. But the Polish officer didn't, and there was also the language barrier. Because there's a difference between being able to understand and express yourself, and speaking the language as it's spoken in the country, without an accent. So officers, especially in London, found themselves working in hotels, cleaning cutlery or helping in the kitchen, there was no training needed for such jobs. So gradually they were de-classed as far as jobs were concerned."

"I remember an advertisement in the paper for a gardener with a cottage and I say, 'Look Stan, cottage, you could be a gardener'. And why not? We went and it was a lovely manor house, beautiful rich people. And the owner saw us and asked us in and he said, 'Well, what are you doing ?'. Stan said, 'Well, I am an officer but I would gladly be a gardener. I would do anything because of that cottage'. And he said, 'No, I wouldn't give you that job, I would be ashamed to give you such a menial job and I would feel very bad if you were my gardener'. So he didn't give us a job. He gave us sherry."

A couple at a dance organised by the Polish community in London, 1961.

BHRU.

"I went to college for Applied Science. I was by myself at that time, might have been different if I'd been married. I'd come home from work about half-past three, get changed, wash, get something to eat and be back at school for six. And I missed going out, going to dances and enjoying myself. So I started neglecting it a bit and once you neglect it, especially in a different language..."

"These British people, you know, had such strange ideas about foreigners in those days. I suppose marriage did help a bit, with our boys marrying English girls, it helped to break that stupid notion that foreigners were so much different to their own people."

Portrait taken in a Yorkshire photographic studio during the 1970s.

BHRU.

"First house together was in Pontefract because we couldn't get a house in Sheffield, they would not give you a room if you had a child. It was very hard to get a room, them days, 1949."

"At grammar school there was a distinct difference. It wasn't anything that you could put your finger on. It was almost a different way of thinking, because we'd been brought up in a certain way. I don't honestly think we had the same sort of freedom as the English kids. My parents were getting on in years and I felt that their point of view was very, very Victorian. Although, having grown up myself now I've realised it wasn't so much Victorian as concern. I don't have many English friends, the friendships that survived are the ones with kids from my own background."

A Polish family visit a photographic studio to celebrate a child's First Communion during the 1970s.

BHRU.

"I had a wife in Poland who, when I was supposed to have died in Russia, she found a boyfriend. After the war, when we found each other, we discussed it quite friendly, but with no possibility of regaining this marriage. We got divorced in Polish law and afterward she married another man and I married another girl."

"I went to a shop, to Marks and Spencer, saw a nice dress, I looked at it and a woman said to me, 'Are you going to buy it?'. I said, 'No. I'm just looking how it's made'. And I went home and made it."

A few years after the death of Stalin in 1953, travel restrictions were eased and small numbers of Poles were able to emigrate to the West. These two women have come from Poland to work at a home for elderly Poles in Chislehurst, Kent.

Tim Smith.

"I worked for a few years in a textile mill in Lodz, and then I met my husband. He didn't want to move to Poland so I came to England in 1981. I was very lonely, I felt absolutely heartbroken. I wanted to go to Poland to see my family. But what happened? Martial law. All borders are closed! The telly showed the soldiers on the street and everything. I was thinking 'Oh God, please don't there be war, all my family are there'. All Christmas, you couldn't phone, you couldn't write, no contact at all. It was really difficult to go through that. That Christmas I'll never forget it."

Holiday photograph taken by a family from Britain visiting Krakow during the 1960s.

BHRU.

"Relatives in Poland and Poles that live in Britain... I think there's a vast difference of thinking. You see, language and culture and everything has progressed in Poland since the war and it's a completely different way of life, whereas here, the émigrés are holding on to something that was pre-war, and of course there's bound to be conflict of opinions. There is a vast difference between them, there's no getting away from that."

"When we went to Poland in 1961, we went to the Embassy to tell them we'd arrived, because if they'd attempted to arrest Leon, the British Consulate could do something about it. The previous Poles who had gone there, that weren't British citizens, they had them taken off and the Consulate could do nothing about it."

Children performing a traditional folk dance at a gathering held during the 1950s.

BHRU.

"The Polish community is very supportive. It keeps Poles together. There are the Ex-Combatants Associations, there is Polish Women Abroad Association, there are all sorts. We try to keep together and try to preserve the traditions etcetera."

"They would have academias where the children at the Polish school would be taught to say various poems, or dances, they'd appear on stage and they'd do their thing. And then you would have a dance in the evening. So again that was another sort of meeting place."

Captain Malewski with a painting of the Battle of Monte Cassino which hangs on the stairs of the Sikorski Museum in London. The museum houses an impressive collection of objects and archives from the Second World War.

Tim Smith.

"Despite the adversity of the War years there was a rich and diverse cultural life. People saw their task as building up a vibrant centre for thought and discussion, continuing the struggle for freedom and acting as a link that explained Poland to the world, and the world to Poland."

Polish sausages being cooked at the summer camp held at Fenton near Newark each year.

Tim Smith.

"They gave me some tripe to eat and I didn't know what to do with it. I like tripe but we make it a different way. She just put it, slap, on the plate and I didn't know what to do with it. But I could see that she put on some salt and vinegar, so I did the same, and I put a piece in my mouth and swallowed it very quickly and she said, 'Do you want another piece?' I said, 'No thank you, I've had enough'. Terrible!"

Polish delicatessen in Bradford in 1985.

Tim Smith.

"Well yes, the delicatessens provided a good meeting place. You didn't have to speak the English language. You went and bought the food that you wanted to eat, your special food."

"I decided to open a continental delicatessen. We got the stock from another Polish man. These shops were just like little clubs. Before they opened it was difficult to buy the continental food. We got the first salami that came from France. On Friday and Saturday the queue started at 8.30 am and we had it all day. Do you know, we could sell anything."

Roman Catholic service being held in Sheffield on Polish Constitution Day, 1999.

Tim Smith.

"The church is absolutely fundamental to everything that happens in Polish society here, and there are few organisations that survive outside the umbrella of a Polish parish. It doesn't mean we're all religious fanatics. The Polish parish priest in Cambridge taught me to play bridge. I've known some who have taught me some of the finer arts of what makes a good vodka. So there are often very worldly, fun priests, not just wishing to dictate doctrine. But nevertheless, it is something that is culturally hugely deep-rooted and it is very, very important."

"You always, on a Sunday, went to church first of all, and then either you had people over at your house for a meal or you would go to somebody else and spend the whole day. And then perhaps pop into church of an evening as well. I suppose to some people it's just a way of life."

Woman at prayer during a Mass held in Todmorden, the home of one of a number of small Polish communities along the Calder valley, West Yorkshire.

Tim Smith.

"The history of the Polish Lutheran church in this country is very interesting in that there are three old pastors who came with the Polish troops in '47, who are still in active ministry, and the other three are us young guys who came from Poland. When you look at the Polish Catholic Church in this country, they've exactly the same situation, half of the priests came from Poland. So Poland, Communist Poland, became an exporter of clergy, very interesting isn't it?"

"I'm Catholic and my husband is Lutheran, and when we wanted to get married I wanted to have the ceremony in the Polish Church, with the Catholic priest, and it was very surprising that the priest didn't want to do that. So we had to go to English Catholic priest, and he didn't see any difficulties at all. That's perhaps why I haven't got much interest in Polish church now, maybe that encounter wasn't very pleasant."

First Communion service being held at the Polish Catholic Mission in Devonia Road, Islington, 1961.

BHRU.

"My first Holy Communion was in one of these London Polish parish churches on Devonia Road, which I know a lot of Polish people attended. The day of my first Communion, apart from having this rather nice white frock and everything, the thing I most vividly remember was the wonderful Polish doughnuts afterwards. After the mass there was this marvellous sort of Communion breakfast for all the children, and apart from the hot chocolate, there is nothing to beat a really good Polish doughnut."

Poles on 'pilgrimage' from all over Britain gathering for an outdoor Mass at Hazelwood Castle, a Roman Catholic monastery near Leeds, 1987.

Tim Smith.

"Nowadays ninety percent of marriages are mixed. Before, marriages were between Polish people. But now, every community is going down and there is no chance for them to find a partner in the community and they are looking for English friends. Every marriage now needs a lot of work from the priest to put together papers, dispensations, because the partners are not usually Catholics. It's nice if the partner is Church of England, or a Christian, but to be honest, most of them are not practising. And for me, a priest, it's a broken heart situation because I know that I am losing these people."

"You know, the world is very, very different now and it's difficult for some of the older generation to accept that times have to change, and that you live in a different country now and whilst everybody's proud of their background, you have to get on with your life in England. Nobody will thank you for being an immigrant all your life, especially when you were born in England, you have to embrace some of the culture here."

Watching a performance by the Polonez dance troupe from Manchester.

Tim Smith.

"I remember going with my brother to Polish school, and the feeling that we both had very strongly was that we didn't want to be there, because it very much made you different to everybody else. It was something that the other children picked up on. 'Why do you have to go to a different school at the weekend, why do you have to learn a silly language like that?'."

"My family were different. I had an English wife and she wasn't interested in Polish language and it was difficult to send the children to the school on a Saturday morning, she never bothered you see."

"We had a professional teacher from Poland who'd taught at University, in fact, teaching these five year olds how to read and write in Polish. And she used to tell us stories, you know, folklore tales and things like this, and it was really good."

"Polish school was a bit of a bind, especially when City were playing at home."

Prayers are read during the festival of Corpus Christi at one of several shrines built around the Polish Parish church in Bradford, 1987. The congregation process between them in a small re-enactment of the pilgrimages that occur in Poland at this time.

Tim Smith.

"They used to worship at St Joseph's on Manchester Road. It was an Irish priest there who allowed them to celebrate Mass. And then, when they had enough funding they bought the building on Edmund Street. They had always had Polish priests here, and now they have them sent over from Poland on sabbaticals. To a lot of second generation people it's quite important, and it's a part of their identity and a part of their culture really."

"We speak Polish at home but the children reply in English. They understand it perfectly but only speak it when they have to. It's idleness basically, plus they're afraid of saying something wrong that people will laugh at, which is stupid really. I just keep saying, 'Speak it, if they laugh at you, tough, just carry on'."

"Certainly my mother has always felt that the language was an essential component of Polishness, and she cared deeply about me having a very high standard of the language because that was the key to the rest of the culture, be it the literature, religion or traditions. But I suppose the other element of that was to be brought up in a home that was Polish Catholic, because the religious aspects of Polish life are very strong and have a bearing on all of the community festivals and traditions."

Demonstration in Warsaw in support of *Solidarnosc*, the trade union Solidarity, which during the 1980s was instrumental in working for Polish independence, which was achieved in 1989.

Janina Struk.

"They remade their lives here and they were happy you know. They got a house, they worked, they brought up kids. I don't think they ever expected to go back to Poland after the first four or five years here, by then it was too late and obvious that they weren't going back to the Poland they remembered before the War. So I think they integrated and accepted it and carried on. And through fundraising they helped Poland in any way they could, medical aid and things like that. And supporting Solidarnosc from the outside. Through their own efforts, in their own way, I suppose they did help to bring a bit of freedom to Poland."

"I supported Solidarity. We used to help people and send letters to the Polish government protesting. Of course, we had to send lots of parcels because people were very poor, they couldn't get anything. So we used to send clothing, we used to collect in Sheffield, even amongst the English people. We were helping them to get food and medicine but they were short of everything then, and there were lorries coming from all over Britain in fact. Sometimes it got into the right hands. A lot of the stuff, the church distributed it, but sometimes it never got in the right place. The army or the police got hold of it, or even Russians that were still there."

Making a toast at a summer get-together in Fenton near Newark, 1999.

Tim Smith.

"Solidarity... I think all Polish people in Bradford supported what was going on. The nice thing for me was that I think it was taken on by the whole of England, people were very supportive. I felt very Polish, I was very proud of what was happening there and very sad to hear of the way people had been treated. It was also very worrying at that time because Polish people weren't quite sure what was happening to their relatives, and naturally we assumed the worst."

"I wished them good luck."

Lwow was home to many of the Poles now in Britain, and is considered by them to be an ancient Polish city. It now lies in Ukraine. The mural on the wall behind celebrates the 'eternal friendship between the Russian and Ukrainian people of the Soviet Union'.

Tim Smith.

"That flame of independence, the desire to maintain the truth, all that was seen as a very strong and binding mission. Now that Poland is in the post-Communist era, I think that currently there is no clear role. Some people of my mother's generation, a few have gone back to Poland. A few people of my generation have set up businesses in Poland, and are therefore living partly there and partly here. But most people who came to England have stayed in England. As have their children and grandchildren. I think we may see more breaking up of the Polish communities, because there isn't that binding cement of needing to keep the voice for independent Poland."

"I was in Poland this spring... now there's big progress. But what's important, people are not the same. I left people who loved our country. Russians, Bolsheviks, when they came, they depraved people. It's not the same."

"We are English subjects now. I'm not thinking for a minute to go back to Poland. My husband said, 'What's the point? Once we've started life here it's no good starting again there'. And I wouldn't go, not at all. Believe it or not, when I go there, apart from the language, I feel I am a stranger somehow."

Farming land in the Carpathian mountains of Galicia, formerly Poland. This area was incorporated into the Soviet Socialist Republic of Ukraine at the end of the War, and collectivised by the Soviets. Since Ukraine won its independence the land is now privately farmed by Ukrainians.

Tim Smith.

"I have not thought about going back. Nowhere to go. No. There are more people that I know in this country. The part of the country I used to live in is Ukrainian now. And there is nobody."

"When you're retired you can go to Poland now to live, but I only lived fifteen years in Poland, I was only a young child. My home is Sheffield you know. I like Sheffield and have lived here for fifty years."

Changing the text on a memorial at Auschwitz concentration camp to acknowledge that the majority of its victims were Jews rather than 'Soviet citizens, victims of the Fascists'.

Janina Struk.

"I tend to actually look to Poland for friendships and Polish identity because, somehow, now that historical truth is emerging, I find it simpler to go there, to absorb the story from Polish museums, Polish libraries, people who are living in Poland, than doing it almost second-hand through the emigre community. And if I'm going to maintain my links for myself, I suspect that's going to be through contact directly with Poland rather than Polish communities here."

"Children, they're a bit different from us. Their Polishness is that they've got cousins in Poland and it's somewhere to go for a holiday. In all honesty that's really all. They learn Polish in school but learn it as a foreign language now, rather than as a first tongue. Mainly they want the 'A' level in it, it comes in handy. They go to Poland but they're not like us where we've got this permanent tie to Poland, where you still do things for Poland, like collect money. They're not like that at all, they were born here, they're English, and I think most children think the same way. That's all it is, it's history to them."

A survivor of the concentration camps at a memorial service in post-independence Poland.

Janina Struk.

"Some experience the return of old memories; of being forcibly uprooted and deported into enemy land; of being compelled to work for the enemy as a slave, or even drafted into his army; of being confined in a concentration camp; separated from loved ones; forced to work in dreadful conditions, and often humiliated for being of a different race. Memories of those dreadful years are still painful today."

Kolyma, Archangielsk, Syberia... a roll call of the places where Poles were taken to slave labour camps in the Soviet Union, on a memorial to those who died there. This memorial is in the Church of St Andrew Bobolas in London.

Tim Smith.

"I know it's fifty years, longer than that, but it was a head down, get on with it mentality when we came here, blot out the past, we've got to survive now. But everything starts coming back to you as you get older. Things that happened that may have laid dormant for years tend to play quite an important role in later life, especially if you've not come to terms with it. My parents' generation, they've coped well with life here. Their own schools for their children, and the churches, and they've always been seen as sort of fairly self-sufficient. But I think, deep down inside, a lot hanker for a life that they left so suddenly. It's the shock, somebody coming and saying, 'Right, you've got half-an-hour, get ready, get some food, some clothing, you're off'."

"Once a refugee, always a refugee they reckon, and I think that's very true. Like my father, he's now eighty-seven. I say to him, 'Oh, wouldn't you like to go back to Poland?'. He says I'm a foreigner here and I would be a foreigner there'. So they have set up their own identities. They remember Poland and they hold these ideals about that country. They're like encapsulated in this timewarp almost."

"Most of my compatriots are still very, very bitter about how the Polish forces were treated. My husband, who was in the Polish army under British command, was not at the Victory Parade, and we felt betrayed. It was very painful and it still is for very elderly people, it still is a wound which is not cleaned at all."

Man who now lives near Lincoln with the deeds of the land and home he lost when he was taken to a concentration camp during the Second World War. This land is now in Lithuania.

Tim Smith.

"My father coped with it better because in his working life he was part of a broader scientific community, as part of his job. Although he always felt Polish, and it was important to him, nevertheless there was this other aspect of his life which has a broader basis in terms of science and research. Whereas for my mother it was really everything, and I don't think she ever got over that loss."

"My mother talked about it a lot. I think the experience of so suddenly losing her home and all her possessions, and the trauma of being deported to Siberia, has altered her whole life irrevocably, and it's something that I think she will never come to terms with. It had a devastating effect on her... She missed her home, her country, her family."

"It is an idealised Poland, I think, because it's a Poland that they, and the people in Poland, no longer have."

Polish scouts at a camp in Lincolnshire looking at photographs taken on a recent trip to Poland in 1999.

Tim Smith.

"I feel that those camps were actually very strong in reinforcing identity. You saw that other children came from similar backgrounds, and the leaders that ran those camps were very, very good at stories, traditions, notions of honour and history, at a level that was appropriate. So they really had a big impact on me, and I used to really look forward to doing that each year."

"I really wanted to break out of the mould and college provided that for me. At the time I needed to sort myself out, because at one stage I was going through an identity crisis. I didn't know where I belonged, whether I was Polish or English, and I came to the conclusion that I was a mixture of both. I was a product of two cultures by the time I'd left college."

"I went back to Poland when I was eighteen, they understood every word I said to them, but they said, 'You talk in a very antiquated language,' which of course it was. It was at least twenty years old. But within a month of being there I'd cottoned on to all the colloquial phrases and everything else. It's a living language in Poland, whereas it's not here. It's become very dormant you know."

Watching a play at the Polish Club in Sheffield.

Tim Smith.

"People at English school just don't understand that Polish Guides are cool. They think it's really sad. They'll go, 'Oh it's so sad'. It's like, 'Well, you don't actually know, so what you going on about?'. But if I say I'm going on holiday with my mates and they go, 'Oh, that's really good,' I say, 'Yeah, it is actually'."

"We're a national minority in this country. A big one but a well-integrated one, and that's something we've worked hard at achieving. But we don't stick out like other groups, we don't have dark skins, we don't wear hats and have long beards or a turban, so it's not so easy to blame us as a group when things go wrong, particularly in times of recession. Not until our children write their names down do people realise they're of Polish descent. Or if they saw them cheering on Poland against England at football. But I'm the same, if Poland play England I'm for Poland, against anyone else I'm on the side of England."

"Youngsters don't put the same value on scout movements. They are British, they were born here, they haven't lost Poland so they haven't got that sentiment. They don't think that Polish language is that important because to them it's a foreign language. But when they grow up they usually complain to their parents, 'Why didn't you insist on teaching me Polish?'. Language is important but children only appreciate it later on in their life."

A woman who lives at Antokal, the home for elderly Poles in Chislehurst, Kent, with a photograph of her and her friends taken in the Middle East during the Second World War.

Tim Smith.

"When I work in residential homes I never hear English people talking about the War and what they've gone through. Never ever. But Polish people, well, maybe their mental health, their physical health, is a result of what they've gone through."

"It is true that a lot of Poles did suffer effects of war and imprisonment, two years' starvation in Siberia or other camps. You shake it off but I think you push it under the carpet and when you get older, it comes out. You reminisce about it."

"All the time we were growing up and going to Polish school and mixing in Polish circles, there was this implicit understanding that we weren't staying, that as soon as Poland was free we were all going back. We were only here temporarily. It was very interesting for me when Poland was liberated. I was thirty-something then, and I still expected my mum and dad to go back. I was really shocked when there was no question about them going back. For them, their children, their grandchildren are here. My mother was nine when she left Poland, and my dad was sixteen, so most of their life was here, yet all the time we were in this Polish bubble. I really expected them to go back, and was taken aback that they didn't. They don't even talk about retiring to Poland, they talk about retiring to the Polish people's home at Penrhos."

Memorial to those members of the Polish Air Force who died during the Second World War, at Northolt in West London.

Tim Smith.

"Often I'll come with friends and we will spend time remembering those whose names are written here."

"I am only one left who was in this regiment from first day to last day. Only I am left now. Last Mohican I call myself."

"Coming here was seen like a safe place, but it wasn't really home, and it never would be home as such. Their home's in their heart, and their heart carries with them the past and what happened before."

FURTHER READING.

Applebaum, A. (London, 1995) Between East and West: across the borderlands of Europe.

Anders, W. (London, 1949) An Army in Exile: The story of the Second Polish Corps.

Ascherson, N. (London, 1987) The Struggle for Poland.

Bauman, J. (London, 1987) Winter in the Morning: A young girl's life in the Warsaw Ghetto.

Carswell, A. (Edinburgh, 1993) For Your Freedom and Ours: Poland, Scotland and the Second World War.

Davies, N. (Oxford, 1981) God's Playground: A history of Poland. Volume I: The origins to 1795. Volume II: 1795 to the present.

Ethnic Communities Oral History Project. (London, 1988) Passport to Exile: The Polish Way to London.

Gill, A. (London, 1994) The Journey Back from Hell: Conversations with Concentration Camp Survivors.

Gula, J. (Dorset, 1993) The Roman Catholic Church in the History of the Polish Exiled Community in Great Britain.

Holmes, C. (London, 1988) John Bull's Island: Immigration and British Society 1971-1971.

Hope, M. (London, 1998) Polish Deportees in the Soviet Union: Origins of post-war settlement in Great Britain.

Hosking, G. (London, 1992) A History of the Soviet Union.

Karpf, A. (London, 1996) The War After.

Krupa, M. (London, 1995) Shallow Graves in Siberia.

Lotnik, W. (London, 1999) Nine Lives: Ethnic conflict in the Polish-Ukrainian borderlands.

Nocon, A. (Oral History Journal, Spring 1996, Vol. 24) A Reluctant Welcome: Poles in Britain in the 1940s.

Rabinowitz, D. (New York, 1979) About the Holocaust.

Suchcitz, A. (London, 1995) Poland's Contribution to the Allied Victory in the Second World War.

Supple, C, and Perks, R. (London 1993) Voices of the Holocaust.

Sword, K. (London, 1996) Identity in Flux: The Polish Community in Britain.

Sword, Davies and Ciechanowski. (London, 1989) The Formation of the Polish Community in Great Britain.

Winslow, M. (Oral History Journal, Spring 1999, Vol. 27) Polish Migration to Britain: War, Exile and Mental Health.

Zamoyski, A. (London, 1987) The Polish Way: A thousand-year history of the Poles and their culture.

Zamoyski, A. (London, 1995) The Forgotten Few: The Polish Air Force in the Second World War.